I0560318

TALK TO ANYONE

OVERCOME SOCIAL ANXIETY AND BUILD STRONGER, MORE MEANINGFUL RELATIONSHIPS WITH NEW PEOPLE

MINDFULMINDS CO

TABLE OF CONTENTS

ACKNOWLEDGMENTS

Writing a book is never a solo journey, and this one is no exception. It's been a collaborative effort filled with support, encouragement, and expertise from many incredible people.

First up, a huge thank you to my family and friends. You've been my rock through this entire process, cheering me on and keeping me grounded. Your belief in me has been the fuel that kept me going, and I can't express how much it means to me.

A special shoutout goes to the amazing team at MindfulMinds Co. Your guidance and insights have been instrumental in shaping this book. You've ensured that the content isn't just meaningful but also something that readers can truly connect with. I couldn't have done this without your expertise.

I also want to give a big thank you to my editors at Publishing Services. Your meticulous attention to detail and unwavering dedication have transformed this manuscript into something I'm genuinely proud of. Your hard work behind the scenes has been nothing short of amazing.

To my mentors, I owe you a debt of gratitude. Your wisdom and insights have been a guiding light, helping to shape the direction of this book. Your advice has left a lasting impact, and I'm so grateful for everything you've shared with me.

And last but certainly not least, thank you to you, the reader. Your curiosity and commitment to learning about emotional intelligence are what give this book its purpose. I hope it offers you the tools and insights you're seeking.

To everyone who has been part of this journey, thank you. Your support has been the cornerstone of bringing this book to life.

INTRODUCTION

Have you ever found yourself at a party, only to find yourself in bewildered wonder about how everyone else seems to walk casually through conversations without a care in the world? Or how about that awkward silence experienced in the elevator? During these moments, do you wish you could just disappear into the floor tiles? If you've ever felt like a deer in headlights during social interactions, you're in the right place. And you're definitely not alone.

Welcome to *Talk to Anyone: Overcome Social Anxiety and Build Stronger, More Meaningful Relationships with New People*. This book was created to empower you with the tools you need to speak up, connect deeply, and feel more confident in any social setting— whether it's a family gathering, a business meeting, or a date.

This book is for everyone. No matter if you're a beginner in the realm of social skills, an introvert who'd rather read a book than attend a social event, or simply someone looking to improve your personal and professional relationships, this book is your new go-to guide. Trust me, we've got your back.

Before we get into the nitty-gritty of what this guide has to offer, let me introduce you to MindfulMinds Co. We are pioneers in the field of Emotional Intelligence. Our team of experts in psychology, mindfulness, and education is dedicated to enhancing emotional well-being. We believe in evidence-based practices to make emotional intelligence accessible and practical for everyone. Together, we were inspired to create a book that helps people overcome social challenges in a way that's both unique and effective.

Let's dive into what makes this book different. First off, it covers both social and professional communication skills. You'll find actionable steps that you can start implementing right away. No fluff, just practical advice. When writing this book, our expert team focused on ease and speed so you can see improvements quickly. But we're not stopping at quick fixes. The strategies you'll find here are designed to bring long-term benefits through sustainable techniques. You'll find that with a little practice, these skills will become second nature, like riding a bike.

In the first few chapters, we'll cover the basics of communication. This includes advice and practical strategies on how to articulate your thoughts clearly and understand body language. Next, we'll get into boosting social confidence with strategies to overcome social anxiety, read body language, start conversations, and sustain them with deep topics that create meaningful connections. We have even included effective exercises to create these conversations and build self-esteem. Then, we'll move on to building meaningful relationships, focusing on deeper connections and techniques for conflict resolution and empathetic listening. We'll look at how to achieve quick and lasting results with easy-to-implement strategies throughout the whole experience as well.

We want you to actively engage with the content with practical exercises, real-life examples, and reflection prompts throughout. Dive in, try out the exercises, and reflect on your experiences. The more you engage, the more you'll gain.

So, let's get started. By the end of this book, I promise you'll feel more confident in your social interactions. You'll have the skills to talk to anyone, build meaningful relationships, and enjoy a richer social life. Are you ready to transform your social interactions and enhance your life? Let's do this!

1

FOUNDATIONS OF EFFECTIVE COMMUNICATION

 The way we communicate with others and with ourselves ultimately determines the quality of our lives.

— TONY ROBBINS

You know that moment when you're at a gathering, and you've just made a brilliant joke that lands perfectly? Everyone laughs, and for a second, you feel like the master of social interactions. But then, someone asks you a follow-up question, and you're suddenly grasping at straws, not knowing what to say, and wishing you could just melt into the background. If you've had this experience, you're not alone. Effective communication can sometimes feel like trying to juggle flaming torches while riding a unicycle. The good news? It doesn't have to be that way. In this chapter, we'll break down the basics of effective communication to make it as simple and straightforward as possible. Let's kick things off with one of the most powerful tools in your communication toolkit: empathy.

THE POWER OF EMPATHY IN CONVERSATIONS

Ever heard the phrase, "Walk a mile in someone else's shoes?" While it's unlikely anyone wants you taking their actual shoes for a stroll, the idea of empathy can transform your interactions. This is because empathy is what turns superficial chit-chat into meaningful conversations. When you genuinely understand where someone is coming from, you build a bridge of trust. Think about it: Would you rather open up to someone who gets you or someone who's just nodding along, waiting for their turn to speak?

Let's take another look at how empathy builds trust using a workplace example. Picture the following scenario for a moment. Your manager notices you've been a bit off lately because you've been working through personal struggles. Instead of brushing it off, they take a moment to ask how you're doing and actually listen. By showing empathy, your manager builds trust, making you feel valued and understood. This trust isn't just touchy-feely stuff; it also boosts workplace morale and productivity. When people feel heard and understood, they're more likely to engage and perform well.

Empathy is also a powerful tool for conflict resolution. Let's say you're having a disagreement with a friend. Instead of jumping to defend your point, you allow yourself a moment to understand their perspective. When doing this, you discover that their frustration isn't really about the issue at hand but something entirely different. By empathizing, you can address the root cause and find a resolution that works for both of you (Aaron Hall, Attorney for Businesses, 2023).

The impact of empathy on communication is profound. It leads to increased emotional connections and enhanced mutual understanding. Think about someone who really listens when you've had a rough day, empathizing with your struggles instead of offering unsolicited advice. Now, imagine how this response to your problems makes you feel cared for and accepted. This kind of empathetic communication strengthens your bonds with others by making everyone feel more connected and supported. Here are a few practical exercises to help you get started with practicing empathy.

Practical Exercise: Building Empathy

1. Empathy Mapping: Empathy Mapping involves creating a visual representation of what someone might be thinking, feeling, saying, and doing in a particular situation. It helps you see things from their perspective more clearly. To engage in this activity, pick a person close to you and think of a conversation you had with them recently. Then, map out what you imagine they were thinking, feeling, saying, and doing in that situation. Write down your thoughts.

2. Role-Playing Exercises: Partner up with a friend and take turns discussing different scenarios and practicing empathy in your responses.

3. Mindfulness Meditation Focused on Empathetic Awareness: Spend a few minutes each day in quiet reflection where you focus on understanding and connecting with the emotions of those around you. Think of your loved ones and close friends and imagine connecting with them on an emotional level.

Incorporating empathy into your daily interactions might seem challenging at first, but with practice, it will become second nature. You'll find that your conversations are richer, your relationships stronger, and your social confidence soaring (Learning Mind, 2018).

ACTIVE LISTENING: MAKING OTHERS FEEL HEARD

There is a stark difference between hearing and listening. Hearing is what your ears do automatically, whereas listening, especially active listening, is what you do with your mind and heart. Active listening is crucial for effective communication because it makes the other person feel genuinely heard and understood. This isn't just important for deep conversations; it's essential in everyday interactions as well.

So, what exactly is active listening? It's far more than just hearing words. It involves being fully present in the conversation, understanding the emotions behind the words, and responding thoughtfully. Imagine you're in a meeting, and a colleague is explaining a complex problem. If you're merely hearing, you might catch some keywords and nod absentmindedly. But if you're actively listening, you're maintaining eye contact, nodding at appropriate moments, and maybe even summarizing their main points to show you're engaged. This kind of listening significantly benefits personal and professional relationships by building trust and mutual respect.

Let's break down the components of active listening. The first is maintaining eye contact. This simple but powerful gesture shows you're paying attention. Then, there's nodding and providing verbal affirmations, like "I see," "Right," or "Absolutely." These small cues signal you're engaged. Next up is summarizing and paraphrasing what the speaker has said. This shows you've been listening and helps clarify any misunderstandings. For instance, if someone says, "I'm really stressed about the upcoming project deadline," you could respond with, "So, you're feeling overwhelmed by the project's timeline?" This gives them a chance to confirm or correct your understanding and keeps the conversation on track.

Now, how do you get better at active listening? Start by avoiding distractions. Put away your phone, close your laptop, and focus entirely on the conversation at hand. It's amazing how much more you can hear when you're not half-listening while scrolling through social media. Another tip is to ask open-ended questions. Instead of "Did you have a good day?" try asking, "What was the highlight of your day?" Asking questions like this encourages more detailed responses and keeps the conversation flowing. For example, a teacher using active listening might ask a student, "Can you tell me more about what's been challenging for you in this subject?" This shows the student that their teacher cares and helps the teacher understand the root of the problem. I encourage you to try some of the following active listening exercises to get started.

Practical Exercise: Active Listening

1. Listening Pairs Activity: Sit down with a friend and take turns talking about a topic for a few minutes while the other person practices active listening. Then, switch roles. I recommend practicing this activity periodically to keep your active listening skills sharp.
2. Reflective Listening Practice: After a conversation, take a moment to reflect on how well you listened. Ask yourself: Did you maintain eye contact? Did you summarize the speaker's main points? Answer these questions as truthfully as possible and use them to improve your listening in your next interaction.

Both exercises give you practice with scenarios that are similar to those you experience in real life, which makes them incredibly valuable. Active listening may sound simple, but it's a skill that takes practice to master. When you make a conscious effort to truly listen, you'll find your conversations becoming more meaningful and your relationships stronger. So, the next time you're in a conversation, remember to listen with your ears, mind, and heart (O'Bryan, 2022).

AUTHENTICITY: BEING GENUINE IN YOUR INTERACTIONS

Have you ever had a conversation with someone who spends too much time crafting their responses and projecting their persona? Before they open their mouth, you can practically see the gears in their head-turning as they think about what they're going to say next. It feels like you're talking to a robot with a well-rehearsed script. Sounds exhausting, right? Well, it is, and I know exactly how you feel. However, being authentic in your interactions can help reduce the number of robotic conversations that you have. Being genuine is also crucial for building trust and credibility in relationships. When you're authentic, you show it; you're a real person with earnest thoughts and feelings. People are more likely to open up to you and share their true selves when they sense you're being genuine. It's like a breath of fresh air in a world filled with pretense.

Authenticity doesn't just impact personal relationships; it's beneficial in professional settings, too. A leader who is upfront about their challenges and admits when they don't have all the answers builds credibility. People respect and trust a leader who shows vulnerability because it makes them relatable. It's the difference between following someone because you have to and following them because you want to. Authenticity in the workplace creates a culture of openness and trust, where employees feel safe to express their ideas and concerns without fear of judgment.

So, how do you embrace your true self without feeling like you're baring your soul to the world? I suggest starting with some self-reflection exercises to understand your values and beliefs. Grab a journal and jot down what matters most to you, like your core principles and what you stand for. These reflections will help you align your actions with your values, making it easier to be authentic. When expressing your thoughts and feelings, I recommend that you strive to be honest yet considerate. You don't want to bluntly state everything that comes to mind, but share your genuine perspective respectfully. Take a leader who leads with authenticity as an example. A leader like this will openly share their vision, acknowledge their team's contributions, and admit when they make mistakes. This kind of leadership inspires trust and loyalty while also creating a positive and productive work environment.

Of course, being authentic isn't always easy. It's normal to have a fear of judgment and worry about what people will think if you reveal your true self. Everyone has insecurities and vulnerabilities. By sharing yours, you create a space where others feel comfortable doing the same. Another potential challenge is balancing authenticity with social norms. You don't want to come across as rude or insensitive. To prevent this, it's important to be genuine while still respecting the context of the situation. Here are some excellent exercises that help with practicing being authentic.

Practical Exercise: Practicing Authenticity

1. Journaling: Write about moments when you truly felt yourself and reflect on how you can bring more of that authenticity into your daily interactions.
2. Role-Play Authentic Scenarios: Partner up with a friend and take turns sharing your thoughts and feelings on various topics. This will help you become more comfortable expressing your true self. You can choose to

talk about any topic that crosses your mind; just make sure that it's genuine!

3. Implement Honesty into Daily Interactions: Make expressing honest opinions in conversations a daily practice. Start small and gradually build up to more significant topics.

The more you practice, the more natural it will feel to be authentic in your everyday conversations. By supporting your authenticity, embracing your true self, being honest, and being genuine will become second nature (Davis, 2019).

UNDERSTANDING EMOTIONAL INTELLIGENCE

Imagine you're at work, and tensions are running high. Deadlines are looming, and everyone's stress levels are through the roof. One manager stays calm, listens to everyone's concerns, and finds a way to keep the team focused and motivated. That's emotional intelligence (EQ) in action. EQ is the ability to recognize, understand, and manage your emotions while also recognizing and understanding the emotions of others. It's made up of five key components: self-awareness, self-regulation, motivation, empathy, and social skills.

Self-awareness is the foundation of emotional intelligence. It's how you understand your emotions, strengths, weaknesses, and triggers. When you're self-aware, you can recognize when you're about to lose your temper or when you're feeling particularly stressed. This allows you to take a step back and choose how to respond rather than reacting impulsively.

Self-regulation is the next piece of the EQ puzzle. It is the basis of managing your emotions, especially in stressful situations. Imagine you've just received some harsh criticism at work. Instead of snapping back or shutting down, self-regulation helps you stay calm, take a deep breath, and respond constructively. You aren't suppressing your emotions when you do this but channeling them in a way that's productive. It puts you in control of your feelings, so you can use them to handle complex situations effectively.

Motivation in the context of emotional intelligence means having a drive to achieve goals for reasons beyond external rewards like money or status. People with high EQ are typically motivated by a deep-seated desire to improve, grow, and accomplish personal and professional goals. They're resilient, optimistic, and committed to their objectives, even in the face of setbacks. Exhibiting this intrinsic motivation often inspires others and creates a positive, goal-oriented environment.

Empathy, as we've touched on previously, is the ability to understand and share the feelings of others. It places you in someone else's shoes and allows you to see the world from their perspective. This component of EQ is crucial for building strong, meaningful relationships. When you empathize with others, you're better equipped to provide support, resolve conflicts, and create a sense of trust and camaraderie. Empathy turns ordinary interactions into opportunities for a deeper connection.

Social skills, the final component of emotional intelligence, are the tools you use to interact effectively with others. This includes everything from casual conversations and conflict resolution to teamwork and leadership. People with strong social skills can work through social and professional networks with ease. They're adept at building rapport, inspiring others, and managing relationships in a way that's both respectful and effective.

Emotional intelligence is critical for effective communication because it leads to better conflict resolution. When you understand your own emotions and those of others, you tend to handle disagreements more effectively. Instead of escalating conflicts, you can find common ground and work towards a resolution. High EQ also improves teamwork and collaboration skills. Here are a few practical exercises that will help you develop and improve your emotional intelligence.

Practical Exercises: Enhancing Emotional Intelligence

1. Practice Mindfulness: Spend a few minutes each day in quiet reflection, where you pay attention to your thoughts and feelings without judgment. Throughout this process, I recommend naming your emotions and allowing them to surface as you feel them. This practice will help you become more attuned to your emotions.
2. Practice Emotion Management: Utilize techniques for managing emotions like deep breathing exercises, taking a walk to clear your head, or simply counting to ten before responding in a heated moment. These strategies will help you regulate your emotions and respond more thoughtfully.
3. Emotional Awareness Journaling: Spend a few minutes each day writing about your emotional experiences, what triggers certain emotions, and how you typically respond. Doing this exercise will help you identify patterns and areas for improvement.
4. Role-Playing Emotional Scenarios: Partner up with a friend and practice responding to various situations, from receiving criticism to handling a disagreement. Make it so that one of you is giving the emotional information and the other is receiving it. Take turns initiating and responding.
5. Practicing Empathy in Daily Interactions: Pay attention to the emotions of those around you and respond with

understanding and compassion in your everyday interactions. For example, if someone gets hurt, you can respond with something like, "Are you alright? Is there anything I can do to help you?"

When you develop your EQ, you'll find yourself navigating social and professional situations with greater ease and confidence (Cherry, 2024).

BUILDING CONFIDENCE THROUGH SELF-AWARENESS

Knowing your strengths and weaknesses allows you to approach social situations with a sense of preparedness and ease. It will also help boost your confidence. This is because when you're aware of what you're good at, you can leverage those strengths in social interactions. Let's say you're a great storyteller but not so good at small talk. Instead of forcing yourself into awkward chit-chat, you can steer the conversation towards a topic where you shine when self-aware. On the flip side, understanding your weaknesses allows you to work on them and turn them into strengths over time. Taking this balanced approach helps you grow personally and socially, making you more adaptable and confident in various situations.

Developing self-awareness isn't as daunting as it sounds. A great place to start is with self-reflection techniques. Take a few minutes each day to think about your interactions. Ask yourself what went well, what didn't, and why. Making this a daily habit will provide valuable insights into your behavior and thought patterns. Another effective method is asking trusted friends or colleagues for their honest opinions about your strengths and areas for improvement. For instance, if one of your friends tells you that you interrupt others too often, you could work on being more patient. This will lead to more engaging and respectful conversations.

Of course, becoming self-aware isn't always a smooth ride. It's tough to admit that you might not be perfect, but overcoming this hurdle is crucial for growth. I would begin by acknowledging that everyone has flaws, and recognizing them is the first step toward improvement. Another common challenge is breaking through self-imposed limitations. It's common to underestimate yourself and hold back because you fear failure or judgment. Pushing past these mental barriers can create new possibilities and boost your confidence. Let's get practical with some exercises to enhance your self-awareness.

Practical Exercise: Building Confidence with Self-Awareness

1. Reflective Journaling: Spend a few minutes each evening jotting down your thoughts and feelings about the day's interactions. Ask yourself questions about what triggered certain emotions and how you responded to them. Write down your answers, identify patterns, and contemplate how you could improve in the future.
2. Mindfulness Meditation: Set aside a few minutes each day to focus on your breath and observe your thoughts without judgment. This will help you become more attuned to your mental state, which will make understanding and managing your emotions come easier.
3. Take a Personality Assessment: Take a personality assessment like the Myers-Briggs Type Indicator (MBTI) online. These tools provide valuable insights into your personality traits and will help you understand how you interact with the world and why you behave the way you do.

Building confidence helps you handle social interactions with greater ease and precision. Understanding your strengths and weaknesses allows you to approach conversations with a sense of preparedness and authenticity (Botelho, 2020).

SETTING THE RIGHT FIRST IMPRESSION

First impressions play a crucial role in forming lasting opinions, and they can significantly impact your personal and professional relationships. Think about it: Would you trust a doctor who greets you with a disheveled appearance and a lackadaisical attitude? Probably not. The same goes for any other interaction. The first impression sets the stage for everything that follows.

So, how do you make a positive first impression? For starters, I would dress appropriately for the occasion. You don't need to wear a tuxedo for a casual coffee meeting, but looking neat and put-together shows you care. Your attire speaks volumes before you even utter a word. Next up is body language. Stand tall, hold your shoulders back, and make eye contact. These simple gestures help convey confidence and openness. Remember, people are quick to judge, and confident body language often makes a world of difference. Take, for instance, a job interviewee who walks in with a firm handshake, maintains eye contact, and smiles genuinely. These small actions leave a lasting positive impression on the employer, increasing the chances of landing the job.

Now, let's break down the critical social components of a strong first impression. Effective communication skills are at the top of the list. Speak clearly and confidently, and actively listen to what others are saying. Positive body language is another crucial element. Smile, make eye contact, and use open gestures to show you're engaged and approachable. Genuine interest and engagement can't be overstated. Show that you're there both physically and mentally. You can do this by asking questions, showing curiosity, and responding thoughtfully. These elements combined create a powerful first impression that will set you up for meaningful interactions. The following are some of my favorite activities for practicing making positive first impressions.

Practical Exercise: Practicing Making a Good Impression

1. Role-Playing First Meeting Scenarios: Partner up with a friend and take turns playing different roles in different introduction scenarios, such as a job interview or a social gathering. Be sure to mix things up and practice both casual and professional greetings. This will help you become more comfortable and confident in these situations.

2. Practicing Your Elevator Pitch: Craft a short, compelling introduction about yourself and practice delivering it smoothly. I recommend creating both a casual and a professional elevator pitch to ensure that you have one that applies to any situation you may find yourself in. This can be particularly handy in networking events where quick introductions are common.

3. Reflect on Your Past Impressions: Take some time to reflect on past first impressions. Think about interactions where you felt you made a strong impression and those where you fell a bit flat. Identify what worked and what didn't, then use these insights to improve your approach.

First impressions are powerful. They can open doors to new opportunities and create lasting connections. By dressing appropriately, using positive body language, and showing genuine interest, you will make a favorable first impression that sets the tone for future interactions. Practice these skills, and soon, they'll become second nature, helping you tackle social and professional settings with ease and confidence. Remember, the first impression is your chance to shine, so make it count (Cherry, 2023).

I understand that breaking out of your shell and putting yourself out there isn't always easy, especially if you have social anxiety. I have experienced struggles with this myself. In the next chapter, we'll discuss how to identify social anxiety triggers and explain how to overcome them.

2

OVERCOMING SOCIAL ANXIETY

Half the world is composed of people who have something to say and can't, and the other half who have nothing to say and keep on saying it.

— ROBERT FROST

Picture this: You walk into a crowded room and instantly feel your heart race, your palms sweat, and your mind go blank. You scan the room for a familiar face, but everyone seems engrossed in their conversations. You can almost hear your inner voice screaming, "Get me out of here!" If this sounds familiar, you're not alone. This is a description of my experience at a social networking event a few years ago. Unfortunately, it also means that you might be grappling with social anxiety. But don't worry. There are ways that you can take social anxiety by the horns and mitigate it in your life. Here, I'll explain how I did this in my life and how you can implement it into yours. Let's begin with the most logical starting point, identifying your triggers.

IDENTIFYING TRIGGERS: UNDERSTANDING YOUR SOCIAL ANXIETY

Understanding what triggers your social anxiety is the first crucial step toward managing it. Think of it like trying to fix a leaky faucet. You can't address the issue if you don't know where the water is coming from. Identifying your triggers allows you to prepare and develop coping strategies by showing you where your anxiety is coming from. Triggers can be internal, like negative self-talk or fear of judgment, or external, such as crowded places or meeting new people.

To identify your triggers, I would start by keeping a daily anxiety journal. Note down situations where you felt anxious, what you were doing, and how you felt. Over time, patterns will emerge, and you'll start to see common triggers. Reflecting on past anxiety-inducing events can also help provide insights. To do this, recall instances when you felt anxious and analyze what might have caused it. It sometimes helps to seek feedback from trusted friends or family when practicing this reflection. They can offer an outside perspective and might notice triggers you're unaware of.

Some common social anxiety triggers include public speaking, attending large social gatherings, and meeting new people. Public speaking is a big one; the thought of standing in front of an audience can make even the most confident person break into a sweat. Meanwhile, large social gatherings can be overwhelming due to the sheer number of interactions happening simultaneously, and meeting new people can trigger anxiety because of the fear of being judged or not making a good impression. Recognizing these triggers will help you prepare and manage your anxiety, especially when handling these kinds of situations.

There are several tools and techniques you can use to track your anxiety triggers over time. I have found mobile apps designed for anxiety tracking to be particularly helpful. These apps allow you to record your feelings and identify patterns easily. Creating a trigger chart is another useful method. To do this, list your triggers and rate the intensity of your anxiety for each one. This visual representation will help you see which triggers are most impactful. For instance, using a mood-tracking app could reveal that your anxiety spikes every time you attend a large social event, helping you prepare for it more effectively (The Recovery Village, 2022). Here are some other ways you can track your anxiety.

Practical Exercise: Anxiety Trigger Tracker

Keeping track of your anxiety triggers will provide valuable insights and help you manage your social anxiety more effectively. Try this simple exercise to identify and track your triggers:

1. Daily Journal: Every evening, spend a few minutes writing about your day. Note any situations where you felt anxious, what you were doing, and how you felt.
2. Trigger Chart: Create a chart with columns for the date, situation, trigger, anxiety level (on a scale of 1-10), and any coping strategies you used. Fill it out daily to identify patterns.
3. Reflection: At the end of each week, review your journal and trigger chart. Look for common triggers and assess the effectiveness of your coping strategies.
4. Feedback: Share your findings with a trusted friend or family member and ask for their observations. They might notice triggers you missed.

Addressing social anxiety starts with understanding what sets it off. By identifying your triggers, you can develop targeted strategies to manage your anxiety and feel more confident in social situations. You've got this (Braman, 2019)!

MINDFULNESS TECHNIQUES TO STAY PRESENT IN CONVERSATIONS

Imagine you're in a conversation, but your mind is wandering all over the place. You're nodding along, but inside, you're thinking about the laundry you forgot to do and the embarrassing thing you said three years ago. This is where mindfulness can be helpful. Mindfulness involves being fully present in the moment. This includes being aware of your thoughts, feelings, and surroundings. It's an incredibly effective tool for managing social anxiety because it helps you stay grounded and focused, which helps reduce the overwhelming flood of anxious thoughts. When you're mindful, you're not worrying about what happened yesterday or what might happen tomorrow. You're fully engaged in the present moment, which makes conversations feel less daunting and more manageable. Staying present can also make your interactions more meaningful by allowing you to connect with others on a deeper level.

Let's get into some basic mindfulness techniques that you can use in social settings. One of the simplest and most effective practices I have found is focused breathing. When you feel anxiety creeping in, take a moment to focus on your breath. Inhale deeply through your nose, hold for a few seconds, and exhale slowly through your mouth. This will help calm your nervous system and bring your attention back to the present moment. Another great technique is body scan meditation. Start at the top of your head and slowly move down to your toes, paying attention to any sensations you feel. This helps you become more aware of your physical presence and reduce tension at the same time.

Mindfulness has a positive impact on social interactions of all kinds. Imagine you're in a difficult conversation with a coworker. Instead of getting caught up in your anxious thoughts, you focus on your breath and stay present. This keeps you calm and collected, allowing you to respond thoughtfully rather than react impulsively. Similarly, mindfulness can enhance your listening skills. When you're fully present, you're more likely to pick up on subtle cues and understand the other person's perspective, making the conversation more interactive and enjoyable.

To further develop mindfulness, you can incorporate some practical exercises into your routine. Guided mindfulness meditation sessions can be a great place to start. There are plenty of apps and online resources that offer guided sessions, making it easy to practice mindfulness anytime, anywhere. Mindful walking is another excellent exercise. As you walk, focus on the sensation of your feet touching the ground, the rhythm of your breath, and the sounds around you (Hoshaw, 2022). Here are a couple more mindfulness exercises that you can incorporate into your life for more practice.

Practical Exercise: Mindfulness in Conversations

1. Mindful Movements: Take a few moments to clear your mind and pay attention to your movements. You can do this as you walk or while sitting down. Once you feel your mind calm and your body relax, return to focusing on the present moment or situation at hand.
2. Mindful Listening: Practice mindful listening by fully focusing on the other person's words. Avoid planning your response while they're speaking. Instead, concentrate on understanding their perspective.

Incorporating mindfulness into your daily routine can help you manage social anxiety and improve the quality of your interactions. By staying present and breaking the cycle of anxious thoughts, you'll find that conversations become less stressful and more enjoyable (Blain, 2023).

BREATHING EXERCISES FOR INSTANT CALM

You know that feeling when your heart races, your palms get sweaty, and it feels like someone just cranked up the thermostat? That's anxiety kicking in, and it can be overwhelming. But did you know that you have a built-in tool to help manage it? Well, you do, and it's your breath. Controlled breathing can be a huge help in mitigating anxiety levels. This is because when you're anxious, your body goes into fight-or-flight mode. Deep breathing helps to counteract this response by calming your nervous system and lowering your stress levels.

Your breath is directly linked to your body's stress response, so learning how to control it can be incredibly powerful. When you take slow, deep breaths, you send signals to your brain to relax and your body to chill out. As a result, your heart rate slows down, your muscles relax, and your mind starts to feel more at ease. It's like hitting the reset button on your stress levels (Blanchfield, 2022).

Now, let's dive into some breathing techniques that you can use to calm yourself during social interactions. First up is box breathing. This technique involves inhaling, holding your breath, exhaling, and holding again, all for the same count. To practice this technique, inhale for four seconds, hold for four seconds, exhale for four seconds, and hold for four seconds. Repeat this cycle a few times. From my experience, box breathing can be particularly useful before entering a social situation because it can help calm your nerves and make you feel more centered and confident quickly.

The 4-7-8 breathing technique is another powerful tool. You can do this by inhaling quietly through your nose for four seconds, holding your breath for seven seconds, and exhaling completely through your mouth for eight seconds. This technique helps to bring your focus to your breath, slowing down your heart rate and promoting a sense of calm (Pugle, 2023). Here's another breathing exercise to help you manage your stress and anxiety.

Guided Breathing Exercise: Diaphragmatic Breathing

1. Find a Comfortable Position: Sit or lie down in a comfortable position. Place one hand on your chest and the other on your belly.
2. Inhale Deeply: Breathe in slowly through your nose, allowing your belly to rise while keeping your chest still. Feel your diaphragm expand.
3. Exhale Slowly: Exhale slowly through your mouth, feeling your belly fall. Your chest should remain relatively still.
4. Repeat: Continue this breathing pattern for a few minutes, focusing on the rise and fall of your belly.

Using these breathing techniques will significantly reduce anxiety and help you feel more in control during social interactions. With regular practice, you'll find that you can summon calm whenever you need it, making social situations less daunting and more manageable (Cronlleton, 2019).

THE POWER OF POSITIVE VISUALIZATION

To describe the power of positive visualization. I would like you to picture the following scenario. You're about to give a presentation in front of a room full of people. Your palms are sweaty, knees are weak, and arms are heavy (sound familiar?). Now, imagine instead that you close your eyes and see yourself standing confidently, delivering your speech flawlessly, and the audience is engaged and nodding along. This technique is called positive visualization, and it's a life-changing way to manage anxiety.

Positive visualization involves creating a detailed and vivid mental image of a successful outcome. The science behind it is fascinating. When you visualize an activity, your brain activates the same neural pathways as it would if you were actually performing it. This means that through visualization, you're essentially rewiring your brain to be more prepared and confident in real-life scenarios.

To practice positive visualization, start by finding a quiet place where you can relax without interruptions. Close your eyes and take a few deep breaths to center yourself. Then, create a detailed mental image of a successful social interaction. Imagine every aspect of the scenario, including the setting, the people, the sounds, even the smells. Use all your senses to make the visualization as vivid as possible. For instance, if you're visualizing a successful presentation, picture the room layout, the expressions on people's faces, the sound of your voice, and the feeling of confidence in your body. This immersive experience will help your brain believe that this situation is possible.

Visualization works wonders for boosting confidence. When you regularly visualize positive outcomes, you train your brain to expect success rather than failure. This leads to increased self-assurance and reduces anticipatory anxiety. Now, imagine that you're a student who visualizes a successful study group session. You see yourself contributing ideas, engaging in discussions, and feeling confident. This mental rehearsal would make you more likely to approach the actual study session with confidence and ease (Sosnoski, 2016). Here's a guided visualization exercise to get you started.

Guided Visualization Exercise: Networking Event

1. Find a Quiet Space: Sit comfortably and close your eyes. Take a few deep breaths to relax.
2. Create a Detailed Image: Imagine you're at a networking event. Picture the venue, the people, and the atmosphere.
3. Engage Your Senses: Hear the buzz of conversations, feel the warmth of the room, and notice the scent of coffee. Visualize yourself confidently approaching a group, introducing yourself, and engaging in a lively conversation.
4. Experience Success: See the positive reactions of others, feel the confidence in your voice, and sense the satisfaction of making meaningful connections.
5. Repeat Regularly: Practice this visualization daily or before any networking event to boost your confidence.

Regularly practicing this positive visualization technique can significantly boost your self-assurance. Trust me, you'll find yourself walking into social settings with your head held high, ready to engage and connect with others in no time (Raypole, 2020).

GRADUAL EXPOSURE: STEPPING OUT OF YOUR COMFORT ZONE

In the past, the thought of mingling with strangers at a party would make my heart race like I'd just sprinted a marathon. However, the concept of gradual exposure helped make these situations less daunting. Gradual exposure is rooted in the principles of exposure therapy, and it involves facing your fears step-by-step rather than diving headfirst into the deep end. This method is effective because it helps desensitize anxiety triggers over time, which helps make them less overwhelming. Gradually exposing yourself to anxiety-inducing situations builds up your tolerance and confidence.

Creating an exposure hierarchy is your first step to gradual exposure. List situations that make you anxious, from least to most challenging. For example, saying hello to a neighbor might be a minor stressor, while attending a large social event could be at the top of your list. Once you've identified these situations, set small, achievable goals for each one. If large gatherings are your kryptonite, your first goal might be to attend a small get-together. Gradually, you can work your way up to more challenging scenarios like large parties or networking events.

Managing discomfort during exposure is crucial. Relaxation techniques, such as deep breathing or progressive muscle relaxation, can be incredibly effective ways to cope with anxiety. Positive self-talk is another powerful tool. Remind yourself that it's okay to feel anxious and that you're taking steps to overcome it. Celebrate your small victories, no matter how minor they may seem. Each step forward is a win. For example, if you manage to strike up a conversation with a stranger at a coffee shop, give yourself a mental high-five. These small celebrations will help boost your confidence and motivate you to keep going.

Let's get into some practical exposure exercises. To start, practice conversations with strangers in low-stress environments. This could be as simple as asking the cashier how their day is going or complimenting someone on their outfit. These small interactions will help build your confidence. Next, try attending small gatherings before tackling larger events. You can do this by joining a book club, attending a small dinner party with close friends, or participating in a community activity. These settings provide a more controlled and comfortable environment where you can practice your social skills. As you become more confident, gradually increase the size of the gatherings you attend. Remember, the goal is to stretch your comfort zone, not to leap out of it entirely. Here's how to create your own gradual exposure plan.

Practical Exercise: Gradual Exposure Plan

1. List Anxiety-Inducing Situations: Write down situations that trigger your social anxiety, from least to most challenging.
2. Set Achievable Goals: For each situation, set a small, achievable goal. For example, if public speaking terrifies you, your first goal might be to speak up in a small meeting.
3. Create an Exposure Schedule: Plan when you will face each situation, starting with the least anxiety-inducing and working your way up.
4. Practice Relaxation Techniques: Use deep breathing or progressive muscle relaxation before and during exposure to manage anxiety.
5. Celebrate Small Victories: After each exposure, take a moment to celebrate your success, no matter how small.

Gradually exposing yourself to anxiety-inducing situations will help you build your confidence and reduce your anxiety over time. Remember, it's a process, and every small step forward is a victory. Keep practicing, and soon, you'll find that situations that once seemed overwhelming become more manageable (Stavraki, 2024).

BUILDING A SUPPORTIVE SOCIAL NETWORK

Social support plays a crucial role in mental health. After all, it offers you a sense of belonging and validation. It's like having a safety net that catches you when you stumble. There are more benefits to having a social network than this, though. It also provides emotional support, practical advice, and a sense of connection that can make facing social situations less daunting.

Building and maintaining a supportive network might seem intimidating, but it's easier than you think. I recommend starting by identifying potential support figures in your life. Look for friends, family members, or colleagues who are empathetic and trustworthy. These are the people who listen without judgment and offer encouragement. Once you've identified them, reach out and make an effort to maintain regular contact. This could be as simple as a weekly phone call, a coffee meetup, or even a text to check in. Consistency is essential for nurturing these relationships.

Sometimes, though, friends and family might not be enough. In these cases, seeking help from professionals can offer the additional support you need. Therapy and counseling provide a safe space to explore your anxiety and develop coping strategies. Cognitive behavioral therapy (CBT), for example, is highly effective for treating social anxiety. It helps you identify and challenge negative thought patterns by replacing them with more positive and realistic ones. Finding the right therapist is critical. I encourage looking for someone who specializes in anxiety and with whom you feel comfortable.

Strengthening social connections can also be achieved through practical activities. Joining support groups or social clubs can provide a sense of community and shared understanding. These groups offer a platform to connect with others who might be experiencing similar challenges, which creates a supportive environment where you can share experiences and advice. Volunteering in community activities is another excellent way to build connections. This is because it helps you meet new people while also giving you a sense of purpose and fulfillment. Furthermore, practicing open and honest communication with friends and family will deepen your current relationships and strengthen your support network. Share your feelings and experiences with them and encourage them to do the same. This mutual openness builds trust, support, and stronger bonds.

Having a strong support system can make the challenges of social anxiety more manageable and provide you with the encouragement and validation you need. Surround yourself with understanding and supportive individuals, and remember that professional help is always an option. By nurturing these connections, you'll find yourself more confident and less anxious in social situations (Braithwaite, 2023).

Once you become more comfortable starting conversations with new people, you'll need some good conversation starters. This is where the next chapter comes in. There, you'll learn how you can start both professional and casual conversations to open the door to new connections. I can't wait to show you how to get started building your social network!

3

MASTERING CONVERSATION STARTERS

 A language is not just words. It's a culture, a tradition, a unification of a community, a whole history that creates what a community is. It's all embodied in a language.

— NOAM CHOMSKY

If you've ever wondered in bewilderment how on earth to begin a conversation with someone naturally, you're not alone. Many people find initiating conversations to be daunting, especially at large social gatherings. But breaking the ice is crucial. It reduces social tension, creates an inviting atmosphere, and can turn an awkward gathering into a memorable event. Think about a party you've attended where the host made everyone feel comfortable. Their ability to break the ice set the tone for the entire evening and made it easier for guests to mingle and enjoy themselves. Here, you'll learn how you can emulate this energy yourself by starting engaging conversations in both casual and professional settings, beginning with the best way to introduce yourself to a stranger: using an icebreaker.

MASTERING THE ART OF THE ICEBREAKER

Initiating a conversation doesn't have to be complicated when you tailor your icebreakers to the type of gathering you're attending. For instance, at a party, a simple "How do you know the host?" can open the door to further conversation. It's a question that everyone can answer and often leads to shared stories and connections. Similarly, you can ask, "Have you tried the [specific food/drink]?" at a dinner party to spark discussions about favorite dishes, cooking tips, and more. Using a shared experience as an icebreaker is particularly effective at reunions. Asking something like, "Remember that crazy thing that happened during our high school trip?" can instantly transport everyone back to a shared memory and dissolve any initial awkwardness. Here are some practical activities that will help get you more comfortable with using icebreakers.

Practical Exercise: Icebreaker Practice

1. Low-Stakes Interactions: Start by practicing icebreakers in everyday situations. Chat with the cashier, the person next to you in line, or a neighbor. Use simple questions like "How's your day going?" or "Have you tried this place before?"
2. Role-Playing Scenarios: Partner up with a friend and take turns role-playing different social events. Practice initiating conversations with various icebreakers and provide feedback to each other.
3. Observe and Reflect: Pay attention to how people respond to your icebreakers. Notice which ones generate positive reactions and which ones fall flat. Reflect on these experiences and adjust your approach accordingly.

By practicing these icebreaker techniques, you'll find it easier to initiate conversations and make social gatherings less daunting and more enjoyable. The more you practice, the more natural it will feel, and soon you'll be breaking the ice like a seasoned pro (Zajac, 2023).

STARTING CONVERSATIONS IN PROFESSIONAL SETTINGS

In professional environments, effective communication is crucial. It's what builds professional relationships and creates networking opportunities. Think about it: That friendly chat at a conference could lead to your next big job offer. So, how do you get the ball rolling in these settings? Tailored conversation starters can make all the difference. At a conference, asking, "What brings you to this event?" can open a world of possibilities. It's a neutral, open-ended question that invites the other person to share their reasons for attending, leading to a more in-depth conversation. Asking a coworker, "What projects are you currently working on?" shows interest in your colleague's work and can lead to discussions about shared goals and challenges in the same way. During networking events, asking fellow attendees questions like, "How did you get started in your field?" is a fantastic way to learn about someone's background and experiences, which creates a pathway to deeper connections.

Context and appropriateness are key when starting conversations in professional settings. This is because understanding the professional setting helps you choose the right icebreaker. A casual chat in the break room differs vastly from networking at a high-stakes industry event. Respecting boundaries and professionalism are equally critical on both ends of this spectrum. You want to come across as interested and respectful, not intrusive. To describe this further, imagine starting a conversation with a senior executive. Asking about their career is appropriate, but diving into personal topics should be off-limits. The important thing is to strike the right balance. Here are a few great ways to practice networking and holding professional conversations.

Practical Exercise: Professional Conversation Practice

1. Networking Event Simulations: Gather a group of friends or colleagues and create a mock networking event. Practice introducing yourself and starting conversations using tailored conversation starters.
2. Practicing Introductions: Take a few minutes each day to introduce yourself to someone new in the office. Use conversation starters like "What projects are you currently working on?" and "How did you get started in your field?"
3. Role-Playing Scenarios: Partner with a friend and role-play different professional scenarios, such as a job interview or a networking event. Practice starting and maintaining conversations and providing feedback to each other.

Starting conversations in professional settings might seem intimidating, but with the right approach, it will become second nature. By practicing these techniques, I guarantee that you'll find it easier to build professional relationships, create networking opportunities, and tackle the complexities of professional communication with confidence and ease (Ramachandran, 2024).

ENGAGING STRANGERS IN CASUAL ENCOUNTERS

Imagine that you're standing in line at your favorite coffee shop, and the person in front of you is wearing a T-shirt from your favorite band. You want to say something, but your inner voice is screaming, "What if they think I'm weird?" Engaging strangers in casual conversation can sometimes feel like walking through a social minefield, but it's an invaluable way to build social skills.

Starting a conversation in everyday situations doesn't have to be complicated. In a café, a simple "This is a great coffee shop, have you been here before?" can break the ice effortlessly. If you're at a library or bookstore, try asking, "What book are you reading?" And anywhere in public, a compliment like "I love your shirt [or another item], where did you get it?" can be a fantastic conversation starter. It's a question that invites the other person to share their interests, and who knows, you might discover a shared passion for something. People generally enjoy talking about their interests and possessions, and such compliments make them feel appreciated as you approach them. Here are some easy ways to start practicing engaging strangers in casual conversation.

Practical Exercise: Casual Conversation Practice

1. Daily Goals: Set a goal to start one new conversation each day. This could be with a cashier, a fellow commuter, someone in a park, or anyone else you come across. Use simple conversation starters like "How's your day going?"
2. Low-Pressure Environments: Practice in places where the stakes are low. Cafes, parks, and public transport are examples of excellent settings for casual conversations. Use questions like "What do you think of this weather?" or "Have you tried the pastries here?"
3. Reflect and Adjust: After each interaction, take a moment to reflect on what went well and what didn't. Adjust your approach based on your observations to improve future conversations.

Engaging strangers in casual encounters can be a fantastic way to build social skills and create unexpected opportunities. Practicing these techniques will make it easier to start and maintain conversations, which will, in turn, make everyday interactions more enjoyable and less intimidating (Morin, 2021).

USING SHARED INTERESTS TO SPARK CONVERSATIONS

Shared interests can be just the thing you need to initiate conversations in casual settings because they create rapport and provide common ground for discussion. Take spending time at a comic book convention as an example. Imagine that you spot someone wearing a T-shirt featuring your favorite superhero at this event. You mention the character and compliment their shirt, and suddenly, you're both deep into a conversation about the latest comic book releases that the character is in. This shared interest sparks the conversation and makes it flow naturally, as both of you are genuinely engaged and excited about the topic.

Identifying shared interests can sometimes seem tricky at first, but it becomes easier with a bit of observation and some open-ended questions. Pay attention to cues like clothing, accessories, or even the books or gadgets people carry. For instance, if you notice someone reading a novel by your favorite author, that's a perfect entry point. Ask, "I see you're reading one of my favorite books. How are you finding it?" This shows your interest and gives the other person a chance to share their thoughts, which creates a natural and engaging conversation.

Another strategy is to ask open-ended questions about hobbies. Questions like "What do you enjoy doing in your free time?" or "Do you have any favorite pastimes?" can also open the door to discovering mutual interests. For example, when you see someone playing Frisbee with their dog at the park, you could say, "Your dog looks like they're having so much fun! Do you play here often?" This potentially leads to a conversation about pets, parks, and perhaps even shared favorite spots for dog walking. Meanwhile, saying something like, "I see you're wearing the T-shirt from one of my favorite bands. Are you a fan?" can open up discussions about concerts, favorite albums, and more. The following are a few simple exercises to help you practice leveraging shared interests to spark new conversations and connections.

Practical Exercise: Leveraging Shared Interests

1. Join Clubs or Groups: Find and join clubs or groups related to your interests, such as book clubs, hobbyist groups, or sports teams. Attend meetings regularly and engage in conversations about your shared interests.
2. Practice at Events: Attend events like book signings, music festivals, or conventions. Use conversation starters related to the event, such as "What's your favorite part of this festival?" or "Have you read any other books by this author?"
3. Observation and Engagement: Pay attention to cues like clothing, accessories, or items people carry. Use these as conversation starters. For example, if someone is wearing a hat from a recent concert, ask, "Were you at that concert too? What did you think of the performance?"

By focusing on shared interests, you create instant rapport and make conversations more engaging and enjoyable. Whether it's a mutual love for a band, a shared hobby, or a favorite author, these commonalities provide a solid foundation for meaningful interactions that build new friendships. So, keep your eyes open for those telltale signs, and don't be afraid to dive into conversations about what you love (Mintz, 2024).

COMPLIMENTS AND OBSERVATIONS AS ICEBREAKERS

Ever noticed how a well-placed compliment can light up someone's face like a kid on Christmas morning? Compliments and observations are powerful tools for starting conversations because they make others feel appreciated and show that you're attentive and interested. When you compliment someone, you're acknowledging their effort, style, or achievement. This instantly creates a positive connection. For instance, complimenting an artist on their work makes them feel valued, and you've just opened the door to a meaningful conversation about their creative process.

Giving genuine compliments, however, requires a bit of finesse. Focus on unique attributes or specific achievements to make your compliments stand out. A generic "Nice shirt" might come off as insincere, but saying, "That's a fantastic pattern on your shirt; it really suits you!" shows that you've paid attention to the details. I would also avoid overused compliments that can feel empty and repetitive. Instead, aim for sincerity and specificity. Complimenting someone's insightful comment beyond "nice work today" can make them feel recognized and valued. Try saying something like, "I really appreciated your point about customer engagement; it gave me a new perspective." This is far more impactful than a simple "Good job."

Observations can also serve as excellent conversation starters. They show that you're present, aware of your surroundings, and approachable. If you're at an outdoor event, a simple "The weather today is amazing, isn't it?" can break the ice and lead to further discussion. Similarly, making an observation about the venue, like "This place has such an interesting layout, don't you think?" can draw people in and make them feel more comfortable sharing their thoughts with you. You can practice making observations and giving compliments with the following activities.

Practical Exercise: Compliment and Observation Practice

1. Daily Compliment Goal: Make it a goal to give at least one genuine compliment each day. Focus on specific attributes or achievements and observe the positive impact they have on the recipient.
2. Observation Practice: Practice making observations in various settings. Use these observations as conversation starters to engage with others. For instance, if you're at a café, you might say, "This place has such a cozy atmosphere, don't you think?"
3. Reflect and Adjust: After each interaction, take a moment to reflect on how the compliment or observation was received. Adjust your approach based on the feedback to improve future interactions.

Using compliments and observations as icebreakers will drastically improve your social interactions. They make others feel valued and show that you're attentive and engaged. So, next time you're in a social setting, remember to look for opportunities to compliment and observe. You might be surprised at how a simple comment can open the door to a great conversation (Barnes, 2023).

Once you have started the conversation, you will need to keep it going. There's nothing worse than starting a conversation only to have it fizzle out prematurely. You'll learn how you can prevent this in the next chapter by asking questions that keep interactions engaging and deepening your connections.

4

SUSTAINING AND DEEPENING CONVERSATIONS

 The first problem of communication is getting people's attention.

— CHIP HEATH

I magine this: You're at your best friend's birthday party, and you're chatting with someone you've just met. The conversation starts off with the usual small talk, but then it fizzles out. You find yourself staring at your drink, wondering how to keep things going without resorting to awkward comments about the weather. Keeping a conversation alive and moving it to a meaningful level is like trying to keep a campfire going. It needs the right kind of fuel. This chapter is all about adding that fuel to your conversations so they don't just survive but thrive. And what is this fuel, you may ask? Well, it's asking open-ended questions, sharing personal stories, and practicing your active listening skills when the other person reciprocates. Going into this, it's important to remember that the best conversations are two-sided. Asking great questions is just as valuable as sharing a great story, joke, or opinion. Let's kick things off with this sentiment in mind by learning how to ask insightful, open-ended questions.

THE ART OF ASKING OPEN-ENDED QUESTIONS

Open-ended questions can be a secret weapon when sustaining and deepening conversations. Unlike yes/no questions, which can stall a conversation, open-ended ones invite detailed responses and promote deeper discussion that flows naturally.

Formulating effective open-ended questions isn't rocket science, but it does require a bit of thought. It's critical to avoid questions that can be answered with a simple "yes" or "no." To avoid this, start your questions with words like "what," "how," and "why." These words naturally invite more elaborate responses. For instance, instead of asking, "Did you have a good weekend?" go for, "How did you spend your weekend?" Asking the second question keeps the conversation going and opens avenues for discovering shared interests.

Let's get more specific with some examples of open-ended questions suitable for various contexts. In a professional setting, you could ask, "What inspired you to pursue your current career?" This question can lead to a discussion about career paths, challenges, and achievements while still not getting overly personal. Meanwhile, asking, "How do you usually spend your weekends?" in a casual setting can reveal hobbies, interests, and activities that you might have in common.

Practice is incredibly helpful for getting the hang of asking open-ended questions. To do this, I recommend role-playing conversations with a friend or family member. Take turns asking open-ended questions and see how the conversation develops. This can help you refine your questioning skills in a low-stakes way. You can also practice by simply using open-ended questions in your daily interactions. For example, when getting to know new colleagues, ask questions like, "What projects are you most excited about working on?" Asking these kinds of questions helps you get to know them better and makes the conversation more engaging for both parties. Here, I've broken down these open-ended questioning practice strategies to make trying them out even more simple.

Practical Exercise: Open-Ended Question Practice

1. Role-Playing Conversations: Partner with a friend or family member and take turns asking open-ended questions. Focus on encouraging detailed responses and promoting deeper discussion.
2. Daily Practice: Incorporate open-ended questions into your daily interactions. For example, when chatting with a barista, ask, "What's your favorite drink to make and why?"
3. Reflection: After each conversation, reflect on how the open-ended questions influenced the discussion. Ask yourself: Did they help sustain the conversation? What could you improve?

Mastering the art of asking open-ended questions through these methods will make your conversations richer and more engaging. You'll move beyond small talk and into deeper, more meaningful discussions naturally, which will also make your social interactions more enjoyable and fulfilling (Vojkovsky, n.d.).

SHARING PERSONAL STORIES TO BUILD CONNECTION

Have you ever shared a good personal story, only to realize that you've suddenly got everyone's attention? People are innately drawn to a good story, so sharing them can be a powerful way to create strong connections. They're so engrossing because they make conversations relatable while also building trust and rapport. When you share a piece of your life, you're inviting the other person into your world. Take, for example, a leader who shares a personal story to inspire their team. By discussing their own challenges and triumphs, they create an atmosphere of trust and camaraderie. This makes the team feel more connected and motivated.

Crafting a compelling personal story is all about how you tell it. You don't have to worry about having a super exciting or extraordinary life. All you need to do is create your story with a clear structure: a beginning, middle, and end to keep it coherent and engaging. Begin with a hook to grab attention, take your listeners through the main events, and end with a resolution or a lesson learned. Including emotions and personal reflections adds depth to your story as well. Talk about how you felt, what you thought, and what you learned from the experience along the way. This emotional layer makes your story more engaging and relatable. For instance, if you're sharing a story about a challenging experience, describe the struggle, the emotions involved, and the eventual outcome. This will captivate your audience and allow them to connect with you on a deeper level.

Let's look at some specific examples of personal stories that you can use as templates in a pinch. Perhaps you once had to give a presentation at work with only a day's notice. You were nervous, but you pulled it off and received positive feedback. Sharing this story can inspire others to face their own challenges with confidence. Another example could be a funny or embarrassing moment that others can relate to. Maybe you once tripped and spilled coffee all over yourself right before an important meeting. Sharing this story can break the ice and make others feel more comfortable around you. I encourage you to practice using your storytelling skills with these activities.

Practical Exercise: Personal Storytelling Practice

1. Writing and Refining Stories: Spend some time writing down different personal stories. Focus on creating a clear structure with a beginning, middle, and end. Include emotions and personal reflections to add depth.
2. Sharing in Small Groups: Practice sharing your stories with small groups of friends or family. Pay attention to their reactions and adjust your storytelling based on their feedback.
3. Public Speaking Clubs: Join a public speaking club or group where you can practice your storytelling in front of an audience. This setting provides valuable feedback and helps you refine your skills.

Sharing personal stories makes conversations more relatable and meaningful. So, the next time you're at a social gathering, don't hesitate to share a piece of your life. You might just find that it's the perfect way to connect with others (Gowin, 2011).

RECOGNIZING AND RESPONDING TO SOCIAL CUES

Ever been in a conversation and felt like something was off, but you couldn't quite put your finger on it? That's the magic (or curse) of social cues. Social cues include body language, facial expressions, and both verbal and non-verbal signals. These cues are essential for sustaining conversations because they tell you how the other person is feeling and what they might be thinking. Imagine you're telling a story, and your friend's eyes start darting around the room. That's a cue that they might be losing interest.

Understanding these signals helps you adjust your approach to social interactions and helps keep your conversations engaging and relevant.

Reading social cues involves more than just noticing when someone yawns. You'll need to interpret subtle signs that indicate interest, disinterest, agreement, or disagreement. For instance, signs of interest can include leaning forward, maintaining eye contact, and nodding. That is because these signals show that the person is engaged and paying attention. On the flip side, signs of disinterest might include crossed arms, looking away, or checking their watch/phone. This basically includes anything hinting that the listener is distracted or in a rush to leave the interaction. Indicators of agreement can be seen in nodding and verbal affirmations like "I see" or "Absolutely." Disagreement might be shown through furrowed brows, shaking the head, or pursing the lips. Recognizing these cues will save you from the dreaded experience of continuing a monologue to an audience who's mentally checked out.

So, how do you respond to these social cues without feeling like you're in a mind-reading competition? If you sense disinterest, try shifting the topic to something more engaging. For example, if someone seems bored during a discussion about work, switch to a lighter subject like weekend plans or a recent movie. This will recapture their attention and make the conversation more enjoyable for both of you. Asking follow-up questions is another way to support engagement. If someone shares a piece of news, ask for more details or their thoughts on the matter. Doing this will keep the conversation going and show that you value their input. For example, if a colleague mentions a new project they're excited about, you could ask, "What are you most looking forward to with this project?" This emphasizes your interest and keeps the dialogue dynamic, making the other person more likely to remain engaged as well. I like using the following exercises to practice recognizing social cues.

Practical Exercise: Social Cue Recognition

1. Observing Interactions: Spend time in social settings, such as cafes or parks, and observe how people interact. Pay attention to body language, facial expressions, and verbal cues. Note how these signals indicate interest, disinterest, agreement, or disagreement.
2. Role-Playing Exercises: Partner with a friend and role-play different scenarios, such as a team meeting or a casual conversation. Practice recognizing social cues and adjusting your communication style accordingly.
3. Reflecting on Real-Life Examples: Think about recent interactions where you noticed social cues, and ask yourself the following questions: What were these social cues? What did they convey? How did you respond? What could you have done differently to improve the conversation?

Recognizing and responding to social cues is a vital skill for sustaining engaging and meaningful conversations. They also help make your interactions go smoother and allow you to connect with others on a deeper level (Watkins, 2021).

HANDLING AWKWARD SILENCES GRACEFULLY

Awkward silences are like the uninvited guests at every social gathering—they show up unannounced and make everyone uncomfortable. But here's the thing: Everyone experiences them. Seriously, even the most seasoned conversationalists aren't immune to this pesky occurrence. It's important to understand that these silences are natural and can serve as opportunities rather than pitfalls. They give you a moment to regroup your thoughts or even shift the conversation to something more engaging.

So, how do you talk through these moments without feeling like you're sinking into quicksand? One effective strategy is to use humor to break the tension. A light-hearted joke or a funny comment about the situation will help ease the awkwardness and make everyone feel more relaxed. For example, if the conversation stalls, you might say something like, "Well, that was a dramatic pause! So, have you ever tried skydiving?" In addition to easing the tension, applying humor like this makes you more approachable and relatable. Another tactic you could use is to ask an open-ended question to restart the conversation. This will shift the focus back to the other person and give them the opportunity to share more to keep the dialogue flowing.

Another approach to tackling awkward silence is to use a conversation restarter. Similar to icebreakers, conversation restarters are specific phrases that help you pivot in a conversation smoothly. For instance, you could say, "I was just thinking about how different this place is from our usual hangouts. What's your take on it?" after a lull in a conversation with a friend. This will re-engage your friend in the conversation and encourage them to share their perspective on the environment around you. Another go-to line is, "This reminds me of a funny story . . ." and then share a light-hearted anecdote. Whether it's about your dog's latest escapade or a mishap you had on your last vacation, personal stories typically reignite the conversation and make it more entertaining. I recommend trying out these activities if you're interested in practicing managing awkward silences.

Practical Exercise: Silence Management Practice

1. Role-Playing Scenarios: Partner with a friend or family member and take turns initiating conversations with planned silences that simulate unplanned and awkward pauses. Practice using humor and conversation restarters to manage these moments.
2. Daily Practice: During regular conversations, intentionally allow for silences, and then use a restarter like, "I was just thinking about what we did last weekend; what's your take on it?"
3. Reflection: After each interaction, reflect on how you handled the silence. Did the humor or restarter work? What could you improve next time?

Awkward silences are inevitable, but they don't have to derail your conversations completely. Using humor, asking open-ended questions, and practicing your responses will help you tackle these moments with ease. Before you know it, you'll be handling awkward silences like a pro and turning them into opportunities for deeper, more engaging conversations (MacLeod, n.d.).

TRANSITIONING FROM SMALL TALK TO MEANINGFUL TOPICS

You know those moments when you're stuck in a loop of small talk, discussing the weather for the umpteenth time, and you're itching to steer the conversation into more meaningful territory? Moving beyond small talk is very fulfilling, and it's crucial for building deeper connections. Transitioning from surface-level chit-chat to more significant topics allows you to create genuine relationships and engage in conversations that are far more satisfying. Imagine being at a networking event, and instead of lingering on pleasantries, you manage to transition into a discussion about your shared passion for environmental sustainability. Suddenly, you're no longer just another face in the crowd; you're someone with whom the other person feels a real connection.

Let's talk about some specific transition statements that can help you move from small talk to more meaningful discussions in real-life scenarios. If you're discussing a recent movie, you could say, "Speaking of movies, it reminds me of how storytelling can really impact our lives. What's a story that's had a significant impact on you?" Saying this shifts the conversation to a deeper level and shows that you're genuinely interested in the other person's experiences. Another example of an effective transition is, "I'm really interested in hearing more about your thoughts on sustainability. Why do you think it's so important?" This statement signals your interest in more profound topics and encourages the other person to share their insights on them. You can practice making transitions in conversations with the following exercises.

Practical Exercise: Conversation Transition Practice

1. Role-Playing with Planned Transitions: Partner with a friend and take turns initiating small talk. Practice using transition statements to move the conversation to more meaningful topics. Focus on making the transitions smooth and natural.
2. Practicing with Friends or Family: During your next casual conversation, consciously try to move from small talk to deeper topics. Use the following transition statement template: "Speaking of [small talk topic], it reminds me of [related deeper topic]."
3. Reflecting on Real-Life Examples: Think about recent conversations where you successfully transitioned from

small talk to meaningful discussion. Reflect on what worked well and what you could improve.

Transitioning from small talk to meaningful topics can transform your conversations, making them more engaging and fulfilling. By using open-ended questions, sharing personal anecdotes, and practicing your transition techniques, you'll find it easier to build genuine connections and enjoy richer interactions. So, the next time you're stuck in a loop of small talk, remember these strategies and take the plunge into more meaningful territory (Colin and Baedeker, 2014).

BALANCING LISTENING AND SPEAKING

Balancing listening and speaking is crucial for keeping conversations engaging and dynamic because it ensures that both parties feel heard and valued. It also leads to a more enjoyable interaction. Mutual engagement is the key to a lively conversation. If one person does all the talking, it can feel like a monologue, leaving the listener feeling disconnected, bored, and possibly even annoyed. On the flip side, the other person might feel like they're talking to a wall if you're too quiet.

So, how do you achieve this balance? One effective strategy is using reflective listening techniques, which involves summarizing or paraphrasing what the other person has said before sharing your thoughts. For instance, if a friend is talking about their challenging week at work, you might respond with, "It sounds like you had a tough week with all those deadlines. How did you manage to get through it?" Taking this approach shows that you're listening and encourages your friend to share more. Being mindful of your speaking time is another great tip. You can do this by paying attention to how long you've been talking and making sure to give the other person a chance to respond. If you find yourself rambling, take a pause and ask for their input. This keeps the conversation balanced and dynamic.

Asking clarifying questions is another great way to show interest and keep the conversation flowing. Questions like "Can you tell me more about that?" or "How did you come to that conclusion?" invite deeper discussion. When it's your turn to speak, share relevant information concisely. Avoid going off on tangents and stay focused on the topic at hand. Here are some activities that are great for practicing balanced communication.

Practical Exercise: Practicing Balanced Communication

1. Practice Active Listening: Continue to practice your active listening skills by asking reflective questions and giving affirming statements like, "I understand that" and "I hear you." Focus on listening to the other person without thinking about what your next response should be.
2. Timed Speaking and Listening Exercise: Set a timer and start a casual conversation with a friend or family member. When you're done speaking, take note of the time and reset the timer when it's the other person's turn to speak. Then, take note of how long they have been speaking for. Continue this process throughout the conversation while taking mental notes. Be careful not to be preoccupied with focusing on the time, though.
3. Reflect on Your Experiences with Active Listening and Timed Speaking and Listening Exercise: Take what you've discovered from the above activities and use it to improve. Ask yourself if you need to spend more time talking, spend more time listening, or refine your active listening skills.

Practicing these techniques will help you find the sweet spot between listening and speaking, which will also make your conversations more engaging and enjoyable for everyone involved. By being mindful of your speaking time, using reflective listening techniques, and practicing active listening, you'll create a more dynamic and balanced interaction. So, the next time you're in a conversation, remember to share the spotlight and listen as much as you speak. Your conversational partners will thank you for it (LinkedIn, 2024).

By now, you've learned the ins and outs of sustaining and deepening conversations, from asking open-ended questions to balancing listening and speaking. These skills will improve your interactions and help you build meaningful relationships. Communication involves more than just speaking and listening, though. You also need to pay attention to nonverbal signals and body language. In the next chapter, we'll explore how you can use these subtle cues to enhance your interactions even further. Stay tuned!

MAKE A DIFFERENCE WITH YOUR REVIEW

SHARE YOUR EXPERIENCE!

"By helping others, we help ourselves."

— UNKNOWN

If *Talk to Anyone: Overcome Social Anxiety and Build Stronger, More Meaningful Relationships with New People* has made a positive impact on your life, your review could do the same for someone else. Many people are seeking guidance to overcome social anxiety and build stronger connections, and your feedback could be just what they need.

At MindfulMinds Co., our goal is to empower as many people as possible to navigate social situations with confidence. To do that, we need your help.

Your review can guide others to the tools they need to improve their social skills and relationships. It takes just a moment, but it could make a big difference in someone's life. Here's how you can help: Leave a review and share how the book has helped you.

Scan the QR Code:

By sharing your thoughts, you're helping others on their journey to overcome social anxiety and connect more deeply with those around them.

Thank you for your support and for helping others improve their lives.

Your friends at MindfulMinds Co.

P.S. If this book has helped you, consider sharing it with someone who could benefit from it too.

5

BODY LANGUAGE AND NON-VERBAL COMMUNICATION

The most important thing in communication is to hear what isn't being said.

— PETER DRUCKER

You know that feeling when you're chatting away with someone, and suddenly you notice their eyes glaze over? Or worse, they start glancing at their watch as if they're waiting for you to finish talking? Yeah, that. It's definitely not fun to come across. This just goes to show that it's not just what we say but how we say it that impacts our interactions. Much of our communication is non-verbal, and understanding this can be life-changing. So, let's get into learning how to read body language and non-verbal signals to help you become a conversation expert, even if you're more of a social wallflower. It's only natural to begin where most people look first in a conversation, the face and the expressions it makes.

READING FACIAL EXPRESSIONS

Facial expressions convey emotions and intentions without us even uttering a word. They help us understand the emotional context and gauge the sincerity of the person we're talking to. Recognizing the subtle differences between facial expressions and understanding what they mean are the keys to understanding someone's true feelings.

Universal facial expressions include happiness, sadness, anger, surprise, fear, and disgust. These expressions are the same across all cultures. If a friend is genuinely happy to see you, their eyes will light up, and their smile will be broad and reach their eyes. On the flip side, if they're faking it, you might notice the smile doesn't quite reach their eyes, and something might feel off. Here are some descriptions of the universal emotions and how you can tell what someone is feeling based on their facial expressions.

Happiness: A happy person will likely smile. Their eyes and eyebrows will be relaxed, though their eyes might be slightly squinted if their smile is wide enough.

Sadness: A sad person will usually frown. You may also notice that their eyebrows are furrowed or knit together and that they're blinking more often than usual. Of course, tears are also a major indicator of sadness.

Anger: Angry people typically furrow or knit their eyebrows and hold their mouths in a tight frown. They might also hold one side of their mouth upwards and keep the other side straight.

Surprise: When surprised, most people open their mouths, raise their eyebrows, and hold their eyes wider than usual.

Fear: People experiencing fear may open their mouths and furrow their eyebrows.

Disgust: A disgusted person will likely avoid eye contact or whatever is disgusting to them. They also may purse their lips or position their mouth in a way that is tight. Their eyebrows may be furrowed as well.

Interpreting facial expressions also involves paying attention to micro-expressions, which are brief, involuntary facial expressions that further reveal true emotions. These can last as little as 1/25th of a second, so noticing them requires keen observation. To practice, try watching a video of someone talking and pausing it at random moments to examine their expressions. Understanding the context is also crucial. For example, a raised eyebrow could indicate surprise or skepticism, depending on the situation.

Cultural variations in facial expressions can throw a wrench into the works. What's considered a friendly gesture in one culture might be seen as rude or inappropriate in another. For instance, while a broad smile might be a sign of friendliness in many Western cultures, it could be perceived as insincere in some Asian cultures. Being mindful of these differences requires cultural sensitivity. When speaking with someone from a different culture, avoid jumping to conclusions based on facial expressions alone, and consider the cultural context to avoid misinterpretations. Here are some more activities that you can try to practice reading facial expressions.

Practical Exercise: Facial Expression Recognition

1. Movie Time: Watch a movie or TV show with the sound off and focus on the characters' facial expressions. Try to guess their emotions based on their expressions alone.
2. Friend Practice: Ask a friend or family member to display different emotions, and practice identifying these expressions. Make it a fun game!

3. Flashcards: Use flashcards with different facial expressions and quiz yourself. This can help you sharpen your skills and recognize subtle cues more quickly.

Improving your ability to read facial expressions will greatly enhance your communication skills. This is because learning to pay attention to non-verbal cues will give you a deeper understanding of the people around you, making your interactions more meaningful and effective (Cuncic, 2023).

THE IMPORTANCE OF EYE CONTACT

Believe it or not, eye contact plays a pivotal role in communication. It builds trust and rapport with the person you're speaking to, shows that you're listening, and demonstrates that you care. This simple act makes the other person feel valued and understood.

Eye contact also shows attentiveness and interest. Think about a time when you were giving a presentation. If you made eye contact with your audience, you likely noticed they were more engaged. This connection is powerful, and it can turn a mundane presentation into a memorable one.

So, how do you use eye contact effectively without coming off as creepy or intense? It's all about balance. You want to maintain eye contact, but not to the point where the other person feels like they're being stared down in an interrogation room. A good rule of thumb is to maintain eye contact for about 60-70% of the conversation. This shows you're engaged without making it uncomfortable for the other person.

Adjusting eye contact based on cultural norms is also crucial. In some cultures, direct eye contact is seen as a sign of confidence and respect, while in others, it might be considered rude or aggressive. For example, in many Western cultures, maintaining eye contact is encouraged, especially in professional settings. However, in some Asian cultures, too much eye contact can be seen as disrespectful. Being aware of these differences will help you interact with people of different cultures more effectively.

That being said, maintaining eye contact can sometimes be challenging, especially if you're dealing with discomfort or anxiety. You might occasionally find it difficult to hold someone's gaze or feel unsure where to look when speaking to a group. If you have a hard time maintaining eye contact, start small. Practice with close friends or family members where the stakes are lower. Gradually, you'll become more comfortable, and it will start to feel more natural. Managing eye contact with multiple people can also be tricky. When speaking to a group, it's essential to spread your gaze around the room to make everyone feel included. Here are some more ways that you can practice making eye contact.

Practical Exercises: Eye Contact

1. Mirror Practice: Stand in front of a mirror and practice maintaining eye contact with yourself. This might feel a bit strange at first, but it's an excellent way to get used to looking into someone's eyes.
2. Conversation Focus: Engage in conversations while consciously focusing on maintaining appropriate eye contact. Start with short interactions, like chatting with a barista or a cashier, and gradually work up to longer conversations.
3. Public Speaking Club: If you have the opportunity, join a public speaking club where you can practice maintaining eye contact with an audience. This is a safe space to experiment and receive constructive feedback.

Practicing these exercises will make it easier to maintain eye contact. Your confidence will grow, and you'll notice a significant improvement in the quality of your conversations (Shafir, 2021).

DECODING GESTURES AND POSTURES

Gestures and postures add further meaning, emotion, and context to our words. Imagine you're in a meeting, and you notice someone sitting with their arms crossed and legs tightly together. That closed posture screams "defensive" or "uncomfortable," even if their words are polite. On the flip side, open gestures, like uncrossed arms and relaxed hands, signal openness and confidence. Recognizing these cues will help you handle conversations more smoothly.

Common gestures and postures can convey a wealth of information. Positive gestures, like nodding, show agreement and encouragement, while negative gestures, such as fidgeting or crossing arms, can indicate discomfort or disagreement. Understanding these subtle signals will help you adjust your approach to social situations in real time. For example, if you're in a meeting and someone is leaning back with their arms crossed, it's a sign they're not on board with what's being discussed. You can then address their concerns directly to make them feel heard and valued.

For example, the meanings of facial expressions, gestures, and posture can vary in different cultures. What's considered a friendly gesture in one culture might be seen as rude in another. For instance, the "thumbs-up" gesture is positive in many Western cultures but can be offensive in some Middle Eastern countries. Being aware of these differences is crucial for effective communication. If you're unsure about a gesture's meaning in a particular culture, it's always better to err on the side of caution and do a bit of research to clear things up before the interaction.

Interpreting body language accurately involves more than recognizing individual gestures and postures. You'll need to understand the context and the cluster of signals being sent at the same time. For instance, someone might cross their arms because they're cold, not because they're defensive. As a result, it's important to always consider the environment and the overall body language before jumping to conclusions. Taking a holistic approach like this will make you a more adept communicator and capable of reading the room like a seasoned pro. Here are some activities you can utilize to make you better at interpreting gestures and posture.

Practical Exercise: Gesture and Posture Interpretation

1. Social Observation: Spend some time in a public place and observe people's body language. Notice how their gestures and postures change in different interactions.
2. Friend Practice: Partner with a friend or family member and role-play various social scenarios. Focus on using and interpreting different gestures and postures.
3. Role-Playing Scenarios: Create scenarios that require different types of body language, such as a job interview, a casual conversation, or a negotiation. Practice recognizing and using appropriate gestures and postures.

Honing your ability to read and interpret gestures and postures will make you a more effective communicator and help you tackle social and professional interactions with greater ease (Ryder, 2021).

USING BODY LANGUAGE TO SHOW CONFIDENCE

Imagine walking into a room with your shoulders slumped and eyes glued to the floor. Now, picture striding in with your head held high and a relaxed, upright posture. Feels different, right? That's the power of body language in action. Confident body language can change both how others see you and how you see yourself. When you carry yourself with confidence, people are more likely to perceive you as competent and trustworthy. This is especially crucial in settings like job interviews, where first impressions really count. Candidates who walk into an interview with a firm handshake, maintain eye contact, and sit with an open posture are more likely to leave a lasting positive impression than those who are fidgeting and avoiding eye contact.

So, how can you adopt confident body language? I recommend starting by maintaining an upright and open posture. Stand tall with your shoulders back and your feet firmly planted on the ground. This makes you look more confident and helps you feel more grounded and stable. Next, use purposeful gestures. I would also avoid fidgeting or making overly exaggerated movements. Instead, use your hands to emphasize points as you speak naturally. Picture a public speaker who uses confident body language to engage the audience. They stand tall, make deliberate hand gestures, and move with purpose. This draws the audience in, making them more likely to listen and engage.

Adopting confident body language isn't always a walk in the park, though. Overcoming self-consciousness is a significant hurdle for many people. You might feel like everyone is watching your every move, scrutinizing your every gesture. But here's a little secret: Most people are too focused on themselves to notice. Practicing in low-stakes environments will help ease this self-consciousness. You can start by practicing in front of a mirror or with close friends. This allows you to experiment and get comfortable without the pressure of a high-stakes situation. Here are some more exercises that can help you develop confident body language.

Practical Exercise: Confident Body Language Practice

1. Power Poses: Spend two minutes before a big meeting or event standing in a power pose. Think Wonder Woman or Superman. Stand with your feet apart, hands on hips, chest out. This will boost your confidence and make you feel more powerful.
2. Role-Playing Scenarios: Partner with a friend and practice scenarios that require confident body language, such as a job interview or a networking event. Focus on maintaining an upright posture, using purposeful gestures, and making eye contact.
3. Networking Event Practice: Attend a networking event and consciously practice using confident body language. Introduce yourself with a firm handshake, maintain eye contact, and stand tall. Notice the difference in how people respond to you.

Incorporating these exercises into your routine will help you become more comfortable using confident body language. Over time, you'll find it easier to project confidence, and your interactions will be more impactful (Cuncic, 2024).

MIRRORING TECHNIQUES TO BUILD RAPPORT

Imagine you're in a conversation where everything just clicks. The other person seems completely in sync with you, and you both leave the interaction feeling surprisingly connected. This magical connection often comes from a technique called mirroring. Mirroring is the subtle act of mimicking another person's body language, gestures, and speech patterns to build rapport. Psychologically, mirroring taps into our innate tendency to feel more comfortable with people who seem similar to us. This typically makes conversations smoother and more enjoyable in both casual and professional settings.

Using mirroring techniques effectively requires a bit of finesse. Subtly mirroring another person's gestures and postures is a great place to start. If they lean forward, you lean forward. If they cross their legs, you do the same. The important thing is to be subtle. You don't want to come off like a mime copying their every move. Next, match the tone and pace of their speech. If they speak slowly and softly, adjust your speech to match. This creates a sense of rhythm and makes the other person feel understood and in tune with you.

Of course, like any technique, mirroring has its challenges. The biggest pitfall is being too obvious. If the other person notices you mimicking them, it can feel manipulative and insincere. The goal should always be to keep it natural and respectful. Avoid exaggerated mirroring, like copying every single gesture or repeating their phrases verbatim. Instead, focus on the overall flow of the interaction. If they laugh, you laugh. If they nod, you nod. Keeping it subtle ensures that the mirroring enhances the connection rather than detracting from it. Here are some ways you can get started with practicing mirroring.

Practical Exercise: Mirroring Practice

1. Mirror Exercise: Spend a few minutes each day in front of a mirror, practicing subtle mirroring of your own gestures and postures. This helps you become more aware of your body language and how to adjust it naturally.
2. Role-Playing with Friends: Partner with a friend or family member and role-play different social scenarios. Focus on using mirroring techniques to build rapport. Switch roles and provide feedback to each other.

3. Team-Building Exercise: If you're in a work setting, incorporate mirroring practice into a team-building exercise. Pair up with a colleague and practice mirroring during a casual conversation. This enhances team cohesion and communication.

Practicing these exercises will help make you more comfortable using mirroring techniques, and they will also make your interactions smoother and more connected. The beauty of mirroring lies in its subtlety. When done right, it can make the other person feel like you're both on the same wavelength, which creates a rapport that's hard to beat (Van Edwards, 2015).

RECOGNIZING INCONGRUENCE IN NON-VERBAL SIGNALS

One minute, you're chatting away with a colleague who's nodding and saying all the right things, but something feels off. You can't quite put your finger on it, but a subtle dissonance between their words and their body language is there. Recognizing incongruence between verbal and non-verbal signals is crucial because mismatches can undermine trust and credibility faster than you can say "mixed messages." For example, imagine your colleague gives positive feedback on your presentation while their eyes dart around the room, and they fidget with their pen. That dissonance screams insincerity, making you question their true feelings.

Learning to spot these incongruences requires keen observation. I would begin by looking for inconsistencies between what someone says and what their body language shows. Are they saying they're excited while their posture is slumped and their arms are crossed? That's a red flag. Context is also important. A smile can mean happiness, but if it's paired with clenched fists, it might indicate frustration. Understanding the context will help you decode these signals more accurately. For instance, if a colleague tells you they're fine but avoids eye contact and has a tense posture, their body language might be screaming for help even though their words are not.

When you spot a mismatch during an interaction, you have a chance to address it directly. This can involve gently probing to understand the underlying issue or simply acknowledging the discrepancy. For example, if someone's words are upbeat, but their body language is closed off, you might say, "You say you're excited about the project, but you seem a bit hesitant. Is there something on your mind?" Taking this approach builds trust and opens the door for more honest communication. Using congruent signals yourself can also help build trust. This is because people are more likely to believe and trust you when your words match your body language. Here are some excellent exercises to help you practice recognizing discrepancies between verbal and nonverbal signals.

Practical Exercise: Recognizing Incongruence

1. Video Analysis: Watch interviews or speeches and analyze the speaker's body language for moments of incongruence. Note inconsistencies between their words and non-verbal signals.
2. Real-Life Practice: During your daily interactions, be mindful of conversations where you sense incongruence. Observe the inconsistencies and consider how you might address them.
3. Role-Playing Scenarios: Partner with a friend or family member and create scenarios with intentional incongruence. Practice identifying and addressing the mismatched signals.

Recognizing incongruence in non-verbal signals will make you more perceptive, which will improve your communication skills. By honing this ability, you'll find yourself holding conversations with greater ease and building more genuine connections (Segal, 2018).

Speaking of building genuine connections, an important part of building healthy relationships is practicing clear, honest, and consistent communication. In the next chapter, you'll learn how to support strong bonds with all types of people by practicing your amazing listening, speaking, and interpreting skills. Let's turn the page and get started!

6

BUILDING AND MAINTAINING RELATIONSHIPS

 It's important to make sure that we're talking with each other in a way that heals, not in a way that wounds.

— BARACK OBAMA

I magine for a moment that you're at a family gathering, and your cousin starts talking about their latest vacation. As they describe the breathtaking views and quirky local customs they discovered on their adventure, you realize you haven't talked to them in ages. In fact, you can't remember the last time you had a meaningful conversation with them. Building and maintaining relationships can feel daunting, especially when life gets in the way. But don't worry. This chapter is all about consistent communication and how it can help you build trust, strengthen bonds, and make you the social butterfly you've always dreamed of being. Let's begin by exploring how consistent communication can build trust.

BUILDING TRUST THROUGH CONSISTENT COMMUNICATION

Trust is the bedrock of any healthy relationship, whether it's with your partner, friends, family, or work colleagues. And consistent communication is the secret to building that trust. This is because consistent communication establishes reliability and dependability. When you make an effort to check in regularly, it shows that you care and are invested in the relationship. It also reduces misunderstandings because you're continuously sharing information and staying on the same page. Think of a manager who regularly checks in with their team. By maintaining consistent communication, they build a sense of trust and reliability, which makes everyone feel supported and understood.

So, how do you keep communication going? I recommend setting aside time for regular check-ins or meetings. Whether it's a weekly coffee date with a friend, a monthly dinner with family, or a daily catch-up call with your partner, having a set schedule ensures that you stay connected. You can even mix things up with emails, texts, and calls. Communication doesn't always have to happen face-to-face.

Transparency and honesty are essential elements of consistent communication. This is because sharing relevant information promptly and addressing issues directly can prevent small misunderstandings from snowballing into major conflicts. Think about it: If you're open about your feelings and intentions, there's less room for assumptions and misinterpretations. Take communicating while working on a group project as an example. If you encounter a problem, addressing it transparently will lead to a quicker resolution and strengthen your working relationship with your colleagues. Here are some practical ways that you can implement and practice consistent, honest communication.

Practical Exercise: Consistent Communication Checklist

1. Set Regular Check-Ins: Schedule weekly or monthly catch-ups with friends, family, or colleagues. Use your phone's calendar to set reminders.
2. Use Various Channels: Mix up your communication methods. Send a text, make a call, or write an email to keep things interesting.
3. Practice Transparency: Role-play scenarios where you need to be open and honest. Discuss a misunderstanding or share your feelings with a partner.
4. Reflect and Adjust: After each interaction, reflect on how it went. Did you feel heard? Was the communication clear? Adjust your approach as needed.

Regular check-ins provide an opportunity to share experiences, discuss any issues, and plan for the future. It's a simple yet powerful way to maintain a healthy and trusting relationship, no matter what the nature of that relationship may be (American Management Association, 2019). By setting these regular check-ins, using various communication channels, and practicing transparency, you'll find yourself tackling social interactions with ease and confidence.

THE ROLE OF EMPATHY IN STRENGTHENING BONDS

Ever had one of those days when everything goes wrong, and you just need someone to listen without offering a five-point plan to fix your life? That's you, needing some empathy. Empathy is the ability to understand and share the feelings of another, which builds mutual understanding and respect. When someone shows empathy, you feel seen and heard. This kind of connection is invaluable, especially during tough times. Think of a time when your friend listened patiently as you vented about your bad day and acknowledged your feelings without judgment. That simple act of empathy probably turned your whole day around.

So, how do you practice empathy in your daily interactions? It starts with active listening and reflective responses. When someone is speaking, really tune in. Put your phone down, make eye contact, and focus on what they're saying. Nod along to show you're engaged, and occasionally summarize what they've said to confirm you understand it. For instance, if a friend says, "I'm really stressed about work," you might respond later in the conversation with, "It sounds like work has been overwhelming for you lately." This shows you're listening and validating their feelings, which is crucial. To validate someone's feelings, you'll need to acknowledge their emotions without trying to fix them. Sometimes, a simple "I understand" or "That sounds really tough" can make a world of difference.

Empathetic communication can help improve your relationships as well. It builds a supportive and caring environment where people feel safe to express themselves. When empathy is present, conflicts and misunderstandings are less likely to escalate. This makes life more comfortable and open in personal relationships. It also creates a collaborative atmosphere in the workplace where everyone feels valued and supported, reducing stress and boosting morale.

Using empathy in conflict resolution can be particularly powerful. Let's say you're working on a team project, and there's a disagreement about the direction to take on the topic. Instead of jumping to defend your viewpoint, you take a moment to understand the other person's perspective. This shows you value their opinion and are willing to consider it, which can help de-escalate conflict and lead to a more productive discussion. Both parties feel heard and understood, and you come to a compromise that satisfies everyone involved. Here are some great exercises that you can use to start building empathy.

Practical Exercises: Building Empathy

1. Empathy Mapping: Imagine yourself in someone else's shoes and think about their thoughts, feelings, and experiences. For example, consider a colleague who seems distant. What might they be going through? How might they be feeling? Apply this exercise to the people in your life and use it to improve your understanding of them.
2. Practicing Empathetic Responses in Conversation: Incorporate empathetic responses into your everyday conversations. The next time someone shares a problem, resist the urge to offer solutions right away. Instead, focus on understanding their perspective and validating their feelings. For instance, if a colleague is frustrated about a project delay, respond with, "I can see why you're frustrated. Delays can be really challenging."
3. Practicing active listening, validating others' feelings, and using empathy in conflict resolution will help you create deeper connections and build a more supportive home and work environment. So, the next time someone shares their feelings with you, remember that sometimes, the best response is simply to listen and understand (Pilla, 2024).

HANDLING DIFFERENT PERSONALITY TYPES

Recognizing and appreciating the variety of personality traits is crucial for building strong relationships because it enhances communication and collaboration by allowing you to tailor your interactions to suit each person better. This helps reduce conflicts and misunderstandings in both personal and professional settings. Imagine a team leader who tailors their approach based on team members' personalities. They might give more direct feedback to someone who thrives on clear instructions while offering more supportive and encouraging comments to someone who is more sensitive. This adaptability makes the team more cohesive and effective.

So, how do you identify different personality types? One useful tool is the Myers-Briggs Type Indicator (MBTI). This tool categorizes people into 16 personality types based on preferences in four areas: introversion/extroversion, sensing/intuition, thinking/feeling, and judging/perceiving. However, while this indicator is incredibly useful, you don't necessarily need a formal assessment to get a sense of someone's personality. You can find out a lot of information about someone's personality by paying attention to behavioral cues and preferences. Is your friend the life of the party, or do they prefer one-on-one conversations? Does your colleague make decisions based on data or gut feelings? These observations will give you valuable insights into how best to interact with them.

Now, let's discuss strategies for interacting with different personality types. Tailoring your communication to suit introverts and extroverts can make a world of difference. If you're dealing with an introvert, give them space to think before responding and avoid putting them on the spot. Meanwhile, engaging extroverts in lively discussions and being prepared for fast-paced exchanges with them is beneficial. You can adjust your feedback methods based on personality traits as well. Some people appreciate direct, no-nonsense feedback, while others might need a gentler approach.

Similarly, if you're managing someone who thrives on specifics, provide clear, actionable feedback and consider giving them specific feedback. Instead of saying, "Great job on the report," try,

"Great job on the report, especially the section where you analyzed the market trends. Your attention to detail really stood out." This kind of tailored feedback shows that you understand and appreciate their strengths, which creates a more positive and productive relationship. You can use the following activities to help you practice communicating with people who have different personality types.

Practical Exercises: Speaking with Different Personality Types

1. Role Playing: Partner up with a friend and take turns playing different personality roles, such as a reserved introvert or a chatty extrovert. Continue to mix it up with some of the other personality differences mentioned in this section and switch roles periodically. This can help you become more comfortable adapting your communication style on the fly.
2. Practicing Adaptive Communication Techniques: Observe how people react to different types of communication and adjust accordingly. For example, if you notice that a colleague responds well to detailed instructions, make an effort to provide more specifics in your interactions with them. Do this in your everyday conversations to gain as much practice as possible.

Understanding different personality types will help you build an environment where everyone feels valued and understood. Whether you're dealing with a friend who loves to chat about their day or a colleague who prefers to get straight to the point, recognizing and adapting to these differences will make your interactions more meaningful and effective. So, the next time you're interacting with someone, take a moment to consider their personality traits and adjust your approach accordingly. You might be surprised at how much smoother your conversations become (Storm, 2017).

EFFECTIVE FOLLOW-UP TECHNIQUES

Imagine that you've just had a fantastic conversation at a networking event. You exchanged business cards, shared a few laughs, and felt a genuine connection with a new work contact. But what happens next? The follow-up. It's the unsung hero of relationship-building. Following up is crucial because it demonstrates reliability and commitment while keeping the lines of communication open. It shows the other person that you value the interaction and are interested in maintaining the connection.

So, how do you follow up effectively? I would start by sending timely and relevant follow-up messages. Timing is everything. Wait too long, and the other person might forget who you are. Send it too soon, and you might come off as desperate. Aim for a sweet spot, which is usually within 24–48 hours. Make your follow-up messages relevant by referencing specific points from your conversation. Personalization is critical. Instead of a generic "Nice to meet you," try something like, "I enjoyed our chat about sustainable architecture at the networking event. Your insights on eco-friendly building materials were fascinating." This shows that you were genuinely engaged and attentive during the conversation.

Different contexts call for different follow-up techniques. After a meeting or event, a brief email or message thanking the person for their time and reiterating the key points discussed can go a long way. For instance, if you had a productive meeting with a potential client, it's great to follow up with a summary of the discussion, highlighting the next steps. This shows that you were attentive and keeps the momentum going. Meanwhile, following up after a successful sales pitch with a timely and personalized message will reinforce their positive impression and keep the conversation going. Acknowledge their specific needs, address any concerns they mentioned, and outline the next steps. This shows that you're proactive and dedicated to providing a solution tailored to their requirements. By following up effectively, you also increase the chances of converting the potential client into a loyal customer.

When it comes to personal milestones like birthdays or anniversaries, a quick check-in or a heartfelt message will strengthen your bond. For example, remembering to send your friend or loved one a message on their birthday every year is a small gesture that shows you care and value their relationship. Here are some excellent practices that will set you up for success when following up with people.

Practical Exercises: Mastering the Follow-Up

1. Set Reminders: Use your phone's calendar or a task management app to schedule reminders for creating and sending follow-up messages. This will ensure that you don't forget to follow up and help you stay organized.
2. Draft Personalized Follow-Up Messages: Create a few follow-up message templates for different scenarios, like after a meeting, a networking event, or a personal milestone. Customize these templates to make them more personal and relevant. For example, after a sales pitch, follow up with a potential client by thanking them for their time and addressing any specific questions or concerns they raised during the pitch. This shows that you were listening and are committed to meeting their needs.

Whether you're nurturing a professional connection or maintaining a personal relationship, consistent and thoughtful follow-ups can make all the difference. By sending timely and relevant messages, personalizing your communication, and practicing regularly, you'll become a follow-up pro in no time (Zucker, 2021).

MAINTAINING LONG-DISTANCE RELATIONSHIPS

Communication barriers, like different time zones and busy schedules, make it challenging to stay connected. This absence of face-to-face interactions can lead to feelings of loneliness and emotional distance. Maintaining a long-distance relationship requires a bit of strategy and a lot of commitment. Setting regular communication schedules is essential. Agree on specific times to talk, such as a daily video call before bed or a weekly virtual date night. Being consistent with this will help create a sense of normalcy and reliability. Technology is your best friend here. Utilize video calls, messaging apps, and social media to stay connected. Seeing each other's faces and hearing each other's voices will make the physical distance feel a bit smaller.

Planning visits and engaging in shared activities are also crucial for keeping long-distance relationships strong. Schedule regular visits to give you something to look forward to and maintain a sense of closeness. During these visits, make the most of your time together by creating memorable experiences. When visits aren't possible, we can participate in virtual activities together. Watch movies simultaneously, play online games, or cook the same meal while video chatting. This will create a sense of togetherness and make the distance more bearable. Here's some more information on how you can support a long-distance relationship.

Practical Exercises: Maintaining Long-Distance Relationships

1. Set Reminders: Create a shared calendar for visits, calls, and activities. This helps you both stay organized and ensures that you have regular touchpoints to look forward to.
2. Establish Regular, Virtual Check-Ins: Set aside time each day or week to connect, even if it's just a quick chat to share how your day went. For example, two friends might schedule a weekly video call to catch up on each other's lives, share stories, and provide support. This consistent effort keeps the friendship strong despite the physical distance.

Maintaining a long-distance relationship isn't easy, but with the right strategies and a commitment to staying connected, it's entirely possible. By setting regular communication schedules, using technology to bridge the gap, planning visits, and engaging in shared activities, you will keep your relationship thriving despite the miles. So, whether you're in a long-distance romance or maintaining a friendship with some physical distance, remember that effort and creativity can turn this challenge into a rewarding experience (Cohan, 2024).

CONFLICT RESOLUTION AND GRACEFUL APOLOGIES

Imagine that you're in the middle of a heated argument with a friend. Voices are raised, feelings are hurt, and it seems like you're both speaking different languages. Conflict in relationships is inevitable, but how you handle it can make or break the connection. As a result, effective conflict resolution is crucial for maintaining healthy relationships. It prevents misunderstandings from escalating and strengthens mutual respect and understanding.

So, how do you resolve conflicts gracefully? I encourage you to practice active listening and open communication as a starting point. When the other person is speaking, really listen to them without planning your rebuttal. Make eye contact, nod, and occasionally summarize what they've said to show you're engaged. Doing this will help you understand their perspective and make them feel heard. At the same time, be honest about your feelings and express them calmly and respectfully. Avoid blaming or accusing language, which can escalate the conflict. Instead, use "I" statements, like "I feel hurt when you cancel plans at the last minute," to express your feelings without attacking the other person.

Finding common ground and compromising is another essential strategy for resolving conflict. To do this, look for areas where you both agree and build from there. It's important to remember that compromise doesn't mean one person always gives in. Rather, you're finding a solution that satisfies both parties. For example, if you're arguing about weekend plans, try to find a middle ground where you can both do something you enjoy. Taking a collaborative approach will resolve the conflict and strengthen the relationship by showing that you're willing to work together.

Now, let's talk about apologies. Offering a sincere and graceful apology is a powerful tool in conflict resolution. Acknowledge your mistakes and take responsibility for your actions. This shows that you're willing to own up to your errors and are committed to making things right. Simply saying "I'm sorry" isn't always enough. Explain why you're sorry and what you'll do to prevent the issue from happening again in the future. For instance, a leader apologizing for a miscommunication can say, "I apologize for the confusion caused by my unclear instructions. In the future, I'll make sure to provide more detailed guidelines." You can practice your conflict resolution skills with the following practical exercises.

Or consider this story about resolving a disagreement with a friend through open communication. Let's say two friends had a falling out over a misunderstanding. Instead of letting the tension fester, one of the friends decides to address the issue directly. They sit down with their friend, actively listen to their perspective, and share their feelings calmly. Through open communication, they both realize that the conflict stemmed from a simple miscommunication, and both apologize for their part in it. By addressing the issue openly and honestly, they resolve the conflict and strengthen their friendship.

Practical Exercises: Resolving Conflict

1. Role-Playing: Partner up with a friend and take turns playing different roles, such as a colleague or family member, to practice navigating conflicts. This helps you become more comfortable and skilled in handling real-life situations.
2. Practicing Sincere Apologies: Write down a few scenarios where you might need to apologize and draft heartfelt apologies for each. This exercise will help you think through your words and ensure that your apologies come across as genuine and thoughtful.

In relationships, conflict is a given, but it doesn't have to be destructive. Practicing active listening, open communication, finding common ground, and offering sincere apologies will help you work through conflicts effectively and strengthen your relationships. Resolving the conflict with grace can transform a potentially negative situation into an opportunity for growth and deeper connection (HelpGuide.org, 2018).

Building and maintaining relationships is all about consistent effort, understanding, and communication. The strategies you've learned in this chapter will help you handle the complexities of human interactions, no matter if they are virtual or in person. Now, let's move on to the next chapter, where we'll explore advanced communication techniques to further enhance your social skills.

7

ADVANCED COMMUNICATION TECHNIQUES

 Communication is your ticket to success if you pay attention and learn to do it effectively.

— THEO GOLD

Have you ever been to a family dinner, and the topic of politics comes up? You feel the tension rising like a pot about to boil over. Everyone has an opinion, and it seems like the conversation could turn into a full-blown argument at any moment. Yeah, I've had it happen to me too. Difficult conversations like these aren't unheard of, and they can be really uncomfortable to work through. But with the right approach, you can handle these tricky situations with grace and tact. This chapter will help you talk in these more difficult conversations and circumstances successfully and come across well without ruffling anyone's feathers. Let's begin by learning how to tackle difficult conversations, shall we?

HANDLING DIFFICULT CONVERSATIONS WITH TACT

Difficult conversations are inherently challenging because they often involve conflict and emotional responses. These interactions require a delicate balance of honesty and sensitivity. Take addressing performance issues with an employee as an example. You'll want to provide constructive feedback without demoralizing them. The potential for conflict in this situation is high, and emotions can run wild. It's easy to see how this conversation could lead to defensiveness or even tears if handled badly. Dealing with conversations like these with tact is crucial to maintaining a positive and productive relationship.

I recommend preparing for difficult conversations by clarifying your objectives and desired outcomes. Ask yourself, what do you hope to achieve from this conversation? Are you looking for a behavior change, an apology, or just want to clear the air? Knowing your goals will help you stay focused. Next, I would anticipate the other person's potential reactions and responses. This doesn't mean you need to script the entire conversation. It's just a good idea to be prepared for different scenarios. When holding the conversation, practice active listening and empathy. Put yourself in the other person's shoes and try to understand their perspective. This will help you approach the issue at hand with compassion and understanding.

Another effective tactic for holding difficult conversations is using "I" statements to express concerns. Instead of saying, "You're always late," try, "I feel frustrated when meetings start late because it affects our productivity." This approach focuses on your feelings rather than blaming the other person. Staying calm and composed under pressure is also essential. Take deep breaths, keep your voice steady, and avoid reacting impulsively. A manager addressing a team member's chronic lateness might say, "I've noticed you've been arriving late frequently, and it's impacting our workflow. Can we discuss how to improve this?" This approach is direct yet respectful, which opens the door for a productive conversation. Role-playing difficult conversations can help you become more comfortable and skilled at handling challenging dialogues. Here's a simple exercise to get you started.

Practical Exercise: Role-Playing Difficult Conversations

1. Identify a Scenario: Choose a difficult conversation you anticipate having. It could be anything from addressing a friend's habit that bothers you to giving feedback to a colleague.
2. Partner Up: Find a friend or family member to role-play with you. Explain the scenario and ask them to play the other person.
3. Practice Active Listening and Empathy: During the role-play, focus on active listening and empathetic responses. Pay attention to your partner's body language and emotions.
4. Use "I" Statements: Practice using "I" statements to express your concerns. Focus on how the behavior affects you rather than blaming the other person.
5. Switch Roles: After practicing the conversation, switch roles and let your partner play you. This will help you see the situation from a different perspective.

Difficult conversations are never easy, but with preparation and the right techniques, you can handle them more effectively. Practice makes perfect, so don't be afraid to role-play and refine your approach (Soeiro, 2021).

PERSUASIVE COMMUNICATION IN PROFESSIONAL SETTINGS

I was once in a meeting, and I needed to convince my team to adopt a new project management tool. Everyone was skeptical, with eyes rolling and arms crossed. Persuasive communication was my golden ticket in this situation, and it will also be yours in every similar circumstance you encounter. At its core, the goal of persuasive communication in professional settings is to build credibility and trust. You need people to believe in you before they can believe in your idea. Understanding your audience's needs and motivations is crucial for building this kind of relationship. For example, if your team is wary of change, framing your pitch around how the new tool will make their lives easier will work wonders. When you connect with what matters most to them, your chances of winning them over increase tenfold.

I encourage you to begin building your professional persuasive messages by structuring your arguments logically. Present your main idea, back it up with solid evidence, and then tie it all together with a compelling conclusion. Using evidence and data to support your claims will turn skeptics into believers. For instance, if you're pitching a new idea via email, include statistics, case studies, and testimonials that highlight the benefits of what you're trying to promote.

It's also important to remember that humans are emotional as well as rational beings. Because of our emotional nature, connecting emotionally with your audience can make your message more compelling. Telling relatable stories can be an incredibly powerful way to do this. Imagine you're trying to persuade your team to adopt a new project management tool, and you share a story about a team that struggled with inefficiencies until they switched to this tool to turn their workflow around. When telling stories like this, I recommend using vivid language to evoke emotions. This will make your message stick. Instead of saying, "This tool will improve efficiency," try, "Imagine a world where your projects run smoothly, deadlines are met with ease, and everyone leaves work on time." Here is a great practical exercise for practicing creating persuasive messages in the workplace to get you started.

Practical Exercise: Crafting Persuasive Messages

1. Choose a Topic: Pick a topic you feel passionate about and want to persuade others about.
2. Structure Your Argument: Outline your main idea, supporting evidence, and conclusion.
3. Gather Evidence: Find data, statistics, or case studies that back up your point.
4. Add Emotional Appeal: Incorporate a relatable story and use vivid language to connect to your audience emotionally.
5. Deliver Your Message: Practice delivering your message in a persuasive speech or email. You can do this by giving your speech in front of a mirror or drafting an email without sending it to anyone.

Practicing persuasive communication can be fun and enlightening. I encourage you to try writing and delivering persuasive speeches on topics you care about. This could be anything from advocating for a new office coffee machine to promoting a more flexible work schedule. Role-playing a sales pitch can also enhance your persuasion skills. To do this, imagine pitching a new product to a potential client. Practice with a friend, focusing on structuring your argument, using evidence, and adding an emotional appeal. This hands-on practice will boost your confidence and make you a more persuasive communicator.

Persuasive communication is a skill you can develop with practice. Building credibility, understanding your audience, crafting compelling messages, and connecting with your audience emotionally will make you a master of persuasion in professional settings. So, next time you're in a meeting and you need to win your team over, remember these tips and techniques. They might just be your secret weapon for turning skeptics into supporters (Birt, 2024).

DEALING WITH REJECTION AND NEGATIVE RESPONSES

Rejection and negative feedback can feel like a punch in the gut. Trust me, I know the feeling. There was a time when I poured my heart into a project only to have my boss tear it apart in a performance review. Ouch. Rejection stings, and it can leave emotional and psychological scars. It can mess with your self-esteem and make you question your abilities. You may start to doubt yourself, wondering if you're good enough. The emotional toll of this can be heavy and lead to feelings of inadequacy and even anxiety. However, rejection is sadly a part of life, and learning how to handle it constructively can make all the difference.

So, how do you handle rejection without cracking under the pressure? I would start by creating and maintaining a growth mindset. This means not seeing rejection as a failure but as an opportunity to learn and grow. It involves understanding that your worth isn't defined by one setback. With this mindset engrained into your mind, seek constructive feedback and apply it. Ask for specific areas where you can improve and use this information to get better at whatever it is you're doing. Think about an entrepreneur who pitches a business proposal and gets turned down as an example. Instead of giving up, they seek feedback on why their proposal was rejected. They then refine their pitch, make improvements, and try again. This resilience and willingness to learn can turn rejection into success.

Responding to negative feedback with grace requires a few key techniques. First, acknowledge and validate the feedback. This doesn't mean you have to agree with everything, but showing that you've heard and understood the feedback is crucial. For instance, if a customer leaves a negative review, acknowledge their experience and thank them for their feedback. Next, ask clarifying questions to better understand the criticism. This will provide valuable insights and help you address the issues more effectively. Imagine receiving negative feedback on a project at work. Instead of getting defensive, you could say, "I appreciate your feedback. Could you provide more details on what specific aspects need improvement?" Responding in this way shows that you're open to learning and improving, which can turn a negative situation into a constructive one. Here's an exercise to help you become more resilient and more comfortable experiencing rejection or negative responses.

Practical Exercise: Building Resilience to Rejection

1. Role-Playing Rejection Scenarios: Find a friend or mentor to role-play different rejection scenarios with you. Practice responding calmly and constructively. Alternate roles every once in a while to gain different perspectives on the situation.
2. Journaling About Past Rejections: Write about past rejections and the lessons you learned from them. Reflect on how you handled the situation and what you could do differently next time.

3. Practicing with a Support Group: Join a support group where you can share your experiences and get feedback. Practicing in a safe environment will build your confidence.

Negative feedback can be a tough pill to swallow, but with the right approach, you can turn it into a valuable learning experience. Acknowledging the feedback, seeking clarification, and maintaining a growth mindset will help you handle rejection with grace and use it as a tool for growth. So, the next time you face rejection, remember that it's not the end of the world. It's just a bump in the road on your path to success (Greenberg, 2021).

CONVERSATIONAL STRATEGIES FOR NETWORKING EVENTS

Networking. Just the word can send chills down your spine if you're an introvert. But let's face it: Networking is crucial for both personal and professional growth. Whether you're at a conference, a job fair, or a casual meet-and-greet, building a network will open doors you didn't even know existed. Take a moment to imagine that you're at a conference and you strike up a conversation with a fellow attendee. Fast-forward a few months, and you're collaborating on a project that skyrockets your career. You would never have met that person or worked on that project without networking.

Making genuine connections is essential to effective networking. Start by setting clear goals and objectives for each event. Know what you want to achieve—whether it's meeting potential clients, finding a mentor, or just expanding your professional circle. Next, prepare an elevator pitch. It's essentially your 30-second commercial that tells people who you are, what you do, and why they should care. A professional successfully networking at an industry event might say, "Hi, I'm Alex, a marketing strategist specializing in digital campaigns. I've helped companies like XYZ increase their online presence by 50%. What brings you to this event?"

Strategies for initiating and sustaining conversations are also critical aspects of successful networking. I always recommend starting by asking insightful questions. Instead of the generic "What do you do?" try "What's the most exciting project you're working on right now?" This shows genuine interest and opens the door for a more engaging conversation. Finding common ground and shared interests can also turn a stiff interaction into a lively discussion. If you notice someone wearing a badge from a company you admire, mention it. "I see you're with ABC Corp. I've always been impressed by their innovation in tech. How do you like working there?" Using conversation starters like these will help you engage with new contacts and make a memorable impression. Here are a few practical exercises to help get you comfortable practicing these helpful networking tips.

Practical Exercise: Practicing Networking Skills

1. Attend Local Networking Events: Start small by attending local meetups or industry events. Practice your elevator pitch and focus on making genuine connections.
2. Role-Playing Networking Scenarios: Partner with a peer and take turns practicing different networking scenarios. One person plays the attendee, and the other practices initiating and sustaining the conversation.
3. Practice Elevator Pitches with a Mentor: Find a mentor or colleague to help you practice your elevator pitch. Get feedback and refine your pitch until it feels natural and compelling.

The more you network, the more natural it will be. By attending events, practicing your pitch, and engaging in meaningful conversations, you'll find yourself becoming more confident and skilled at networking in no time (The Muse, 2018).

COMMUNICATING IN GROUP SETTINGS

Ever been in a meeting where everyone's talking at once, and you're just sitting there, trying to figure out if it's safe to jump in? I know I have. The unique dynamics of group settings present both communication challenges and opportunities. On the one hand, you've got multiple perspectives and ideas, which can lead to rich, productive discussions. On the other, it's easy for voices to get lost, for conflicts to arise, and for the conversation to go off the rails. Picture leading a group discussion in a team meeting. You're managing the flow of multiple people in a conversation and need to ensure everyone has a chance to speak while still keeping the discussion on track.

Effective group communication starts with facilitating inclusive and balanced discussions. This means not letting the loudest voice dominate and making sure even the quietest team member feels comfortable sharing their thoughts. To achieve this, you'll need to create an environment where everyone feels valued. You can do this by encouraging participation from all group members by asking open-ended questions and inviting quieter individuals to share their insights. For example, if you're managing a brainstorming session, you might say, "I'd love to hear from those who haven't spoken yet. What are your thoughts on this idea?" This approach will bring in diverse perspectives and create a sense of inclusion and collaboration.

Group conflicts are inevitable, but they don't have to derail the conversation. Managing these conflicts requires a calm and strategic approach. Start by mediating disagreements and finding common ground. Listen to each side without taking sides yourself, and look for points of agreement that can serve as a foundation for resolution. You can encourage collaborative problem-solving by framing conflicts as shared challenges that the group can tackle together. Imagine a team leader managing a brainstorming session where two colleagues have opposing views. Instead of letting the argument escalate, the leader might say, "Both of you bring up valid points. Let's see if we can find a solution that incorporates the strengths of both ideas." This approach will resolve the conflict and strengthen the team's ability to work together. You can practice these group communication skills with these helpful activities.

Practical Exercises: Practicing Group Communication

1. Practicing Group Discussions and Meetings: Gather a few friends or colleagues and simulate a group meeting. Take turns leading the discussion, encouraging participation, and managing any conflicts that arise. Make changes to your approach based on their feedback and your experiences.
2. Role-Play Group Conflict Resolution Scenarios: Come up with a scenario where team members disagree on the direction of a project. Practice mediating the discussion, finding common ground, and guiding the group toward a collaborative solution. This exercise helps you develop the skills and confidence needed to handle real-life group communication challenges.

With the right strategies and practice, you can tackle group interactions with confidence. You can make group settings less intimidating and more productive by facilitating inclusive discussions, managing conflicts effectively, and practicing your skills. These tips and techniques might just be the key to turning a chaotic discussion into a harmonious collaboration (Kitch, 2023).

TAILORING YOUR APPROACH FOR DIFFERENT CULTURES

Cultural differences shape our communication styles, and understanding these nuances is crucial for effective international interactions. Being sensitive to these cultural differences will enhance your cross-cultural relationships and can make or break international projects. Working with international colleagues on a project requires understanding their cultural norms. Misinterpreting a gesture or tone can lead to misunderstandings and tensions. Respecting cultural differences encourages collaboration and builds stronger, more effective teams.

To identify cultural differences, start by observing and researching different cultural behaviors. Look for cues in how people interact, their body language, and their communication styles. Researching these cultural norms will provide valuable insights. For example, in some cultures, maintaining direct eye contact is a sign of confidence, while in others, it can be perceived as aggressive. As you can probably imagine, knowing the difference between how the person you're talking to perceives eye contact will dramatically alter the tone and success of the interaction. Asking respectful questions about cultural preferences can also help. If you're unsure how to address someone or what gestures are appropriate, it's okay to ask politely. A simple "How do you prefer to be addressed?" or "Is there anything I should know about your cultural practices?" shows respect and a willingness to learn.

It's crucial to adapt your communication style to suit different cultural contexts by adjusting your language, tone, and formality. In some cultures, formal language and a respectful tone are essential, while in others, a more casual approach is appreciated. Being mindful of non-verbal cues and body language is also important. For example, in a multicultural team meeting, you might notice that some colleagues prefer not to interrupt, while others are more vocal. Adapting your communication style to accommodate these differences can help create a more inclusive environment. This might mean allowing more pauses in conversations or encouraging quieter team members to share their thoughts. Here are a couple of activities that will help you get more comfortable with cross-cultural communication.

Practical Exercise: Practicing Cross-Cultural Communication

1. Participate in Cultural Exchange Programs or Events: This can provide hands-on experience with different cultures. This is because engaging with diverse groups and communities helps you practice and refine your cross-cultural communication skills. To do this, look up local or online events that celebrate a wide range of cultural experiences and actively participate in them.
2. Role-Play Cross-Cultural Communication Scenarios: Partner up with a friend or colleague. One person can play the role of someone from a different culture, while the other practices adapting their communication style. This exercise can highlight areas where you might need to adjust your approach and help you become more comfortable with cross-cultural interactions.

Tailoring your approach to different cultures will help you avoid faux pas, build meaningful connections, and create mutual respect. The next time you're working with international colleagues or engaging in a cross-cultural interaction, remember these tips and techniques. They might just be the key to turning a potential cultural clash into a harmonious collaboration (Jain, 2024).

Developing and building on your communication skills doesn't end here. In the next chapter, you'll learn even more ways to support your self-growth and long-term communication development. All you need to do to set yourself up for successful future interactions is turn the page and get started.

8

PRACTICAL EXERCISES AND LONG-TERM DEVELOPMENT

 I'm a great believer that any tool that enhances communication has profound effects in terms of how people can learn from each other, and how they can achieve the kind of freedoms that they're interested in.

— BILL GATES

Have you ever tried to learn a new language or pick up an instrument? The first few weeks are a whirlwind of excitement and progress. But then, like clockwork, the initial enthusiasm fades, and you're left wondering what you should do next. Mastering communication skills is no different. Daily practice and consistency are crucial for continuing to enhance your communicative abilities. In this chapter, you'll discover all the best ways to support continuous growth on your path to successful interactions. Let's begin by establishing an effective daily communication practice routine.

DAILY COMMUNICATION PRACTICE ROUTINE

Daily practice is essential for mastering communication skills because it builds and reinforces new habits. Like most other things in life, the more you practice communication, the more it becomes second nature. Consistent effort also typically leads to incremental improvement, making each day a step closer to your communication goals.

Creating a daily communication routine doesn't need to require monumental changes to your schedule. I would start by setting simple, specific, and achievable goals. Maybe aim for a 15-minute conversation practice session each day. Allocate a dedicated time slot for this practice and commit to it. Even just this simple and short communication practice can lead to significant improvements over time. The idea is to make it a part of your daily routine. Eventually, it will become second nature.

Now, let's talk about what you can do during these practice sessions. Engaging in small talk with strangers can be a great place to start. It might feel awkward at first, but it's a great way to practice your conversational skills in low-stakes environments. All you need to do is compliment someone's outfit while waiting in line or ask the barista how their day is going. Another powerful exercise is practicing active listening during daily interactions. When your colleague talks about their weekend, really listen. Nod, make eye contact, and ask follow-up questions. And if you're looking to spice things up, use daily interactions at work to practice open-ended questions. Instead of asking, "Did you have a good weekend?" you could try, "What was the highlight of your weekend?" These small tweaks can make a big difference. Mix and match these ideas to prevent the practice from becoming stale and to continue refining more than one communication skill. Maintaining motivation and consistency when developing your communication skills can be challenging, but it's not impossible. Here are some goals that you can set to keep you motivated as you continue to develop them.

Practical Exercise: Daily Communication Goals

1. Set Achievable Goals: Decide on a specific goal for your daily practice. For instance, aim to engage in one meaningful conversation or meet a new person that day. You can set a new goal each day or have the same goal a few days in a row. The choice is yours!
2. Allocate Time Slots: Identify a consistent time each day for your practice. It could be during your lunch break, commute, or before bed. Whatever works for you!
3. Track Your Progress: Use a habit-tracking app or a simple chart to mark each day you practice. Celebrate each small victory, like completing a week of consistent practice or achieving a milestone.
4. Find an Accountability Partner: Pair up with a friend or colleague who's also working on their communication skills. Practice together and keep each other motivated.

By incorporating these exercises into your daily routine, you'll find that your communication skills will improve steadily. Before you know it, you'll have a bounty of social confidence and meaningful relationships on your hands (Dunn, 2018).

SELF-REFLECTION AND JOURNALING PROMPTS

Using self-reflection to enhance self-awareness and overall emotional intelligence is crucial for continuous improvement in communication skills because it helps you gain insights into what you're doing well and where you might need a little extra help. You start to understand not just how you react to things but why.

Journaling is one of the most effective ways to practice self-reflection. It's like having a conversation with yourself where you can share and analyze anything your mind can think of. You can start this practice by setting aside dedicated time for journaling. This could be in the morning with your coffee or at night before bed. Any time that works for you is fine! The important thing is to make it a consistent part of your routine. I recommend using prompts to help focus your thoughts and make the writing process feel less daunting.

To get you started, here are some specific journaling prompts. Ask yourself, "What went well in my conversations today?" This will help you focus on the positives and recognize your strengths. Another good prompt is, "What challenges did I face in my conversations today, and how did I handle them?" This question encourages you to think about difficult moments and how you responded. It's a great way to identify areas for improvement. Lastly, try, "How can I improve my listening skills?" This prompt will keep you focused on becoming a better listener, which is a key component of effective communication.

Integrating journaling into your daily life doesn't have to be a chore. Keep your journal in a convenient location, like your nightstand or desk, so it's always within reach. Setting reminders for journaling time can also help make it a regular habit. You can use an alarm on your phone or a sticky note as a reminder. If you're more tech-savvy, using a digital journaling app can offer convenience and flexibility as well. This is because they give you the option to journal anytime, anywhere, without carrying around a physical notebook. Here is a breakdown of a practical journaling exercise to get you started.

Practical Exercise: Self-Reflection Journaling with Prompts

1. Find a Quiet Space: Choose a comfortable and quiet place where you can focus without distractions.
2. Choose a Time: Decide on a regular time for journaling, whether it's in the morning, during lunch, or before bed.
3. Use Prompts: Start with prompts like "What went well in my conversations today," "What challenges did I face, and how did I handle them," and "How can I improve my listening skills?"
4. Write Freely: Allow yourself to write freely without worrying about grammar or punctuation. The goal is to capture your thoughts and reflections, not write a perfect essay.
5. Review and Reflect: Periodically review your journal entries to identify patterns and areas for improvement. This is also a great way to measure your growth.

Making journaling a part of your daily routine will make self-reflection become second nature. Over time, these small reflections will lead to significant changes and make you a more effective, empathetic, and confident communicator. Grab that journal, find your cozy spot, and start reflecting—you might be surprised at what you discover (Raypole, 2016).

LEVERAGING TECHNOLOGY FOR SOCIAL SKILLS DEVELOPMENT

Imagine for a moment that you're at home in your pajamas, sipping on your favorite cup of coffee and practicing your public speaking skills. No, this isn't a dream—it's the magic of technology. Today, technology should be an integral part of improving your social skills. With access to a wide range of resources and tools, you can practice and refine your communication skills without ever leaving your house. Think about it: Video conferencing platforms, language learning apps, and online forums all provide opportunities for virtual communication practice and feedback. Take, for example, someone who uses video conferencing to practice public speaking. They join virtual meetings, present their ideas, and receive real-time feedback, all while sitting in the comfort of their own home.

So, how can you make the most of these technological marvels? I recommend getting started by using language learning apps to improve your verbal skills. These apps often come with interactive exercises, pronunciation guides, and even virtual conversation partners. Social media websites and apps are also great tools for networking practice. Platforms like LinkedIn or online forums can help you engage in discussions, ask questions, and share your insights. This allows you to practice your communication skills and build your professional network simultaneously. I have also found using a speech analysis app to be incredibly beneficial for improving presentation skills. These apps analyze your speech, provide feedback on your pacing, tone, and clarity, and offer suggestions for improvement. It's like having a speech coach available 24/7.

Integrating technology into your daily practice doesn't have to be overwhelming. I would start by setting specific goals for your technology use. For example, you could aim to spend 20 minutes each day on a language learning app or participate in one online forum discussion per week. Here is how you can implement technology into your regular communication practice in a way that's easy and practical.

Practical Exercise: Tech-Savvy Communication Practice

1. Set Specific Goals: Decide on clear objectives for your technology use. For example, aim to join one virtual meeting per week to practice public speaking.
2. Choose Your Tools: Identify the digital tools that best suit your needs. This could be a language app, a video conferencing platform, or an online forum.
3. Allocate Time: Dedicate specific time slots for your tech-based practice. Whether it's 15 minutes each morning or an hour every Sunday, consistency is key.
4. Track Your Progress: Use a habit-tracking app or a simple checklist to monitor your progress. Celebrate small victories, like completing a week of consistent practice.

Leveraging technology for social skill development can be incredibly effective. It offers flexibility, a wealth of resources, and endless opportunities for practice and feedback. Balancing screen time with face-to-face interactions is also crucial, though. While technology is a fantastic tool, real-life interactions are irreplaceable. Make sure to practice your skills in both virtual and real-world settings. By integrating these tools into your daily routine and balancing virtual and in-person interactions, you'll find yourself becoming more confident and proficient in your communication skills. So, go ahead, fire up that laptop, and start practicing (Block, 2024). You've got this!

CREATING A PERSONAL GROWTH PLAN

A personal growth plan is your path to setting clear goals and milestones, tracking your progress, and staying motivated along the way. It's essential for continuing to develop your communication skills long-term. Creating a personalized growth plan starts with identifying your specific communication goals. Ask yourself, what do you want to achieve? Maybe you want to improve your public speaking skills, become a better listener, or feel more comfortable in social settings. Once you've pinpointed your goals, break them down into actionable steps. Let's say a student wants to improve their public speaking skills. Their plan might include joining a public speaking club, practicing speeches in front of a mirror, and seeking feedback about their public speaking from peers. Breaking goals into smaller, manageable tasks makes them less daunting and more achievable.

A well-rounded growth plan includes various components. Daily and weekly practice routines are crucial for reinforcing new habits. I also recommend incorporating self-reflection and feedback mechanisms to gain insights into your progress. For instance, include role-playing exercises in your growth plan to simulate real-life scenarios. This could involve practicing job interviews with a friend or engaging in mock networking events. Diversifying your practice methods will help you develop a more comprehensive skill set. Think of it like cross-training for athletes —different exercises target different muscles, leading to overall improvement. The same is true for practicing different communication skills.

Maintaining and adjusting your growth plan is key to its effectiveness. To do this, regularly review and update your plan to ensure it stays relevant and aligned with your evolving goals. Celebrate achievements and milestones to stay motivated. For example, a professional might adjust their growth plan based on feedback from a mentor. If they receive feedback that their presentations lack engagement, they can incorporate new strategies to make them more interactive. This continuous refinement keeps the plan dynamic and effective. Here are some useful instructions to help you create and maintain your very own communication growth plan.

Practical Exercise: Personalized Growth Plan

1. Set Clear Goals: Identify specific communication goals you want to achieve, such as aiming to improve public speaking skills.
2. Break Down Your Goals: Divide your goals into actionable steps. If improving public speaking, steps might include joining a public speaking club, practicing speeches, and seeking feedback on your public speaking skills.
3. Incorporate Practice Routines: Establish daily and weekly routines to practice your skills. Include activities like role-playing and self-reflection.
4. Track Progress: Use a journal or app to track your progress and celebrate your goal milestones. Regularly review and update your plan based on feedback and achievements.

Setting clear goals, breaking them down into actionable steps, and incorporating diverse practice methods will ensure that you progress steadily. Additionally, regularly reviewing and adjusting your plan will keep it relevant and effective (Sutton, 2023).

BUILDING A SUPPORTIVE COMMUNITY FOR ONGOING LEARNING

Having a network of supportive individuals is crucial for continuous learning and development in communication skills. It provides encouragement and motivation, which will help you push through moments of doubt. It also offers diverse perspectives and feedback, allowing you to see your blind spots and grow in ways you never imagined.

Take my own experience as an example. I once joined a networking group for career development. Initially, I felt out of place and unsure of how to handle a room full of strangers. However, as I began to engage with the group, I received valuable feedback and support, which made the experience feel less daunting and more exciting. I experienced the benefits of a supportive community first-hand, and I know you can, too. So, how do you build and engage with a community like this? Well, I would start off by looking for clubs, forums, or social media groups focused on communication skills. Participating in workshops and seminars can also be incredibly beneficial because they provide opportunities to learn from experts and connect with like-minded individuals. Attending communication skills meetups is yet another fantastic way to practice and learn in a social setting. These meetings often include activities, discussions, and exercises that help you hone your skills. The more you immerse yourself in these communities, the more you'll gain from them.

Being part of a supportive community requires you to contribute as much as you receive. You can contribute to your community by sharing your knowledge and experiences. This can actually be incredibly rewarding. Offer constructive feedback to others, and don't be afraid to share your own challenges and successes. This will help create a culture of mutual support and continuous learning. Plus, it's a great confidence booster. The more you contribute, the more you benefit from the community.

Offering constructive feedback is another way to contribute. When someone shares their experience or practice, provide thoughtful and encouraging feedback. This helps them develop their communication skills and strengthens your own under-standing at the same time. Here are some more ways that you can engage with your community and create a supportive environment for further developing your communication skills.

Practical Exercises: Engaging with Your Community

1. Lead a Workshop: Collaborate with some communication experts and put on a workshop that focuses on building communication skills. Incorporate activities, games, and engaging presentations to keep the event both fun and informative.
2. Create an Online Forum: Create a forum that encourages everyone to practice and develop their communication skills together. Select a popular platform like Facebook or LinkedIn to create the forum or group, and select trusted admins or moderators to help you manage the online community as it grows. Remember to actively engage with the group and encourage others to do the same in a way that's constructive and respectful.

Building and engaging with a supportive community allows you to create a rich environment for continuous learning and development. The encouragement, motivation, diverse perspectives, and feedback you receive will propel you to new heights in your communication skills. And by contributing to the community, you help others grow while reinforcing your own learning. It's a win-win situation that makes the learning process more enjoyable and effective. All you need to do is find your community and start building those supportive connections. You'll be amazed at how much you can achieve together (Miller, 2020).

We are now approaching the end of this life-changing guide, but it's not over yet. I still have a few tips and tricks left up my sleeve! Next, we'll go over the key components of this book and explain how you can continue supporting your communication and social skill development even after you finish the final page. So, whenever you're ready, let's keep going!

CONCLUSION

So, here we are, standing at the finish line of our marathon toward effective communication. I would like to take a moment to congratulate you on how far you've come. Remember when you first opened this book? You were probably a little nervous. Throughout this book, I encouraged you to get out of your comfort zone and begin habits that might not necessarily have come naturally to you at first. But look at you now! You've successfully worked through the challenges that come along with social anxiety, initiating small talk, and holding meaningful conversations. Let's take a moment to recap the highlights of this amazing adventure and remember just how far you've come since first opening this book.

We kicked things off by laying the foundations of effective communication. We discussed the power of empathy, active listening, and authenticity. You learned to recognize the importance of emotional intelligence and how to build confidence through self-awareness. You became a more emotionally intelligent and reflective version of yourself, allowing you to grow into the fantastic person you are today. From there, we moved on to overcoming social anxiety, identifying your triggers, and mastering mindfulness techniques to stay present in conversations. We also explored the magic of positive visualization and gradual exposure, all while building a supportive social network. Hopefully, at that point, engaging in new conversations didn't seem quite as daunting, and managing anxiety became easier.

After that, we tackled conversation starters and learned to break the ice in various settings. You now know how to engage strangers, use shared interests to spark conversations, and ask questions that lead to deeper discussions. We also dove into the nuances of sustaining and deepening these conversations by mastering the art of asking open-ended questions and sharing personal stories to build connections.

Understanding body language and non-verbal communication was another key chapter in this book. You can now read facial expressions, use eye contact effectively, and decode a variety of gestures and postures. You've also learned how to use body language to show confidence and build rapport through mirroring techniques. Not only that, but you discovered how you can recognize incongruence in non-verbal signals as well.

Building and maintaining relationships was another major milestone you experienced along this path to developing communication skills. You discovered the importance of consistent communication, practicing empathy, and navigating different personality types when starting and maintaining all types of relationships. Effective follow-up techniques and maintaining long-distance relationships also became a part of your social toolkit, along with expert conflict resolution skills.

Advanced communication techniques rounded off and completed our experience together. You now know how to handle difficult conversations with tact, use persuasive communication in professional settings, and deal with rejection and negative responses. Networking events no longer daunt you, and you're skilled at communicating in group settings and tailoring your approach for different cultures.

So, what have we learned? The major takeaway is that communication is an art, not a science. It requires practice, patience, and a willingness to step out of your comfort zone. You've gained all the knowledge you need to become an expert communicator, but the work doesn't stop here.

Now, it's time for some action! Don't let this book gather dust on your shelf. Use it as a springboard to dive into real-life communication practice. Continue to set daily goals to engage in meaningful conversations and practice active listening, join local clubs or online forums to expand your social network, and don't forget to keep a journal. It's always beneficial to reflect on your progress and look for areas needing improvement.

Mastering communication is a lifelong task. There will always be new situations, new people, and new challenges. But with the tools and techniques you've acquired, you're more than equipped to handle them. Remember, every conversation is an opportunity to learn, grow, and connect. So, embrace the awkward silences, the nervous jitters, and the occasional faux pas. They are all part of the social experience.

Knowing the ins and outs of successful communication techniques is one of the best ways to enhance your personal life and professional career. It can open doors, mend relationships, and build bridges. It can also turn strangers into friends and friends into lifelong companions. I encourage you to go out there, armed with your newfound skills, and make the world a little smaller, one conversation at a time.

From me and all of us at MindfulMinds Co., thank you for allowing us to be part of your path to greatness. We believe in the transformative power of effective communication, and we're excited to see how you'll use it to benefit your life and the lives of those around you. Remember, the world is full of potential connections just waiting to be made. All it takes is a few words to get started.

REFERENCES

Aaron Hall, Attorney for Businesses. "The Power of Empathy in the Workplace: Building Trust and Engagement," September 13, 2023. https://aaronhall.com/insights/teamwork/the-power-of-empathy-in-the-workplace-building-trust-and-engagement/.

American Management Association. "How to Use Communication to Build Trust and Inspire Loyalty, as Well as Lead Effectively," January 24, 2019. https://www.amanet.org//articles/how-to-use-communication-to-build-trust-and-inspire-loyalty-as-well-as-lead-effectively/.

Barnes, Mia. "60 (Non-Cheesy) Get To Know You Icebreakers For Your Team." Science of People, April 4, 2023. https://www.scienceofpeople.com/get-to-know-you-icebreakers/.

Birt, Jamie. "13 Effective Ways To Persuade Others in the Workplace." Indeed, June 28, 2024. https://www.indeed.com/career-advice/career-development/how-to-persuade-people.

Blain, Tiara. "How Does Mindful Communication Impact Mental Health?" Verywell Mind, May 8, 2023. https://www.verywellmind.com/mindful-communication-definition-principles-benefits-how-to-do-it-7489103.

Blanchfield, Theodora. "Want to Feel More Relaxed? Try These Deep Breathing Techniques." Verywell Mind, September 22, 2022. https://www.verywellmind.com/the-benefits-of-deep-breathing-5208001.

Block, Martin. "Social Skills Mastery: Effective Techniques for Adults with Developmental Disabilities." forbesaac, June 18, 2024. https://www.forbesaac.com/post/social-skills-mastery-effective-techniques-for-adults-with-developmental-disabilities.

Botelho, Gabrielle. "Building Self-Confidence Through Self-Awareness." HR Exchange Network, November 30, 2020. https://www.hrexchangenetwork.com/employee-engagement/columns/building-self-confidence-through-self-awareness.

Braithwaite, Kisha. "Cultivating a Strong Social Support Network." Psychology Today, November 7, 2023. https://www.psychologytoday.com/us/blog/resilient-you/202311/cultivating-a-strong-social-support-network.

Braman, Lindsay. "Trigger-Tracker Worksheet for Mental Health Journaling and Self-Advocacy - LindsayBraman.Com," December 27, 2019. https://lindsaybraman.com/trigger-tracker-worksheet/.

Cherry, Kendra. "Emotionally Intelligent People Have These 10 Traits in Common." Verywell Mind, January 31, 2024. https://www.verywellmind.com/what-is-emotional-intelligence-2795423.

Cherry, Kendra. "First Impressions: Everything You Need to Make a Good Introduction." Verywell Mind, March 14, 2023. https://www.verywellmind.com/make-a-good-first-impression-7197993.

Cohan, Deborah J. "9 Proven Ways to Maintain a Long-Distance Relationship." Psychology Today, January 2, 2024. https://www.psychologytoday.com/intl/blog/social-lights/202401/9-surefire-ways-to-nurture-a-long-distance-relationship.

Colin, Chris, and Rob Baedeker. "How to Turn Small Talk into Smart Conversation." Ideas. Ted. Com (blog), July 28, 2014. https://ideas.ted.com/how-to-turn-small-talk-into-smart-conversation/.

Cronleton, Emily. "10 Breathing Techniques for Stress Relief." Healthline, April 9, 2019. https://www.healthline.com/health/breathing-exercise.

Cuncic, Arlin. "12 Ways to Have More Confident Body Language." Verywell Mind, January 16, 2024. https://www.verywellmind.com/ten-ways-to-have-more-confident-body-language-3024855.

Cuncic, Arlin. "How to Read Facial Expressions." Verywell Mind, March 28, 2023. https://www.verywellmind.com/understanding-emotions-through-facial-expressions-3024851.

Davis, Tchiki. "Develop Authenticity: 20 Ways to Be a More Authentic Person." Psychology Today, April 15, 2019. https://www.psychologytoday.com/us/blog/click-here-happiness/201904/develop-authenticity-20-ways-be-more-authentic-person.

Dunn, Nikki. "Daily Exercises to Improve Your Communication Skills." Skill Incubator, July 5, 2018. https://skillincubator.com/daily-exercises-to-improve-your-communication-skills/.

Gowin, Joshua. "Why Sharing Stories Brings People Together." Psychology Today, June 6, 2011. https://www.psychologytoday.com/us/blog/you-illuminated/201106/why-sharing-stories-brings-people-together.

Greenberg, Barbara. "10 Ways to Manage Rejection." Psychology Today, December 8, 2021. https://www.psychologytoday.com/us/blog/the-teen-doctor/202112/10-ways-manage-rejection.

HelpGuide.org. "Conflict Resolution Skills," November 2, 2018. https://www.helpguide.org/articles/relationships-communication/conflict-resolution-skills.htm.

Hoshaw, Crystal. "What Mindfulness Really Means and How to Practice." Healthline, March 29, 2022. https://www.healthline.com/health/mind-body/what-is-mindfulness.

Jain, Anurag. "Ten Strategies for Effective Cross-Cultural Communication: A Comprehensive Guide." Digicrusader: Digital Business Coach (blog), March 9, 2024. https://digicrusader.com/ten-strategies-effective-cross-cultural-communication/.

Kelly, Mj. "100 Communication Quotes to Remind You How Powerful It Is." Goalcast, July 9, 2021. https://www.goalcast.com/communication-quotes/.

Kitch, Bryan. "5 Best Practices for Better Group Communication." Mural, May 10, 2023. https://www.mural.co/blog/group-communication.

Learning Mind. "What Is Empathic Communication and 6 Ways to Enhance This Powerful Skill - Learning Mind," August 28, 2018. https://www.learning-mind.com/empathic-communication-skills/.

Lebow, Hilary. "Good Question... 45+ Deep Conversation Starters." Psych Central, March 22, 2015. https://psychcentral.com/health/deep-conversation-starters.

LinkedIn. "How Do You Balance Listening and Speaking When Leading a Meeting or a Presentation?" June 28, 2024. https://www.linkedin.com/advice/0/how-do-you-balance-listening-speaking-when-leading.

MacLeod, Chris. "Ways To Deal with Awkward Silences In Conversations." www.succeedsocially.com, n.d. https://www.succeedsocially.com/awkwardsilences.

Miller, Andrew. "Creating Effective Professional Learning Communities." Edutopia, January 3, 2020. https://www.edutopia.org/article/creating-effective-professional-learning-communities/.

Mintz, Kyla. "Great Engaging Conversation Starters to Break the Ice Every Time." Kumospace, May 23, 2024. https://www.kumospace.com/blog/conversation-starters.

Morin, David, and Daniel Wendler. "How to Start a Conversation (Without Being Awkward)." SocialSelf, October 10, 2021. https://socialself.com/start-conversation/.

O'Bryan, Amanda. "How to Practice Active Listening: 16 Examples & Techniques." PositivePsychology.com, February 8, 2022. https://positivepsychology.com/active-listening-techniques/.

Pilla, Dave. "Empathy: The Conduit of Connection." Psychology Today, January 2, 2024. https://www.psychologytoday.com/us/blog/interconnected/202312/empathy-the-conduit-of-connection.

Pugle, Michelle. "10 Useful Breathing Techniques to Try Anywhere." Verywell Health, October 31, 2023. https://www.verywellhealth.com/breathing-techniques-8382890.

Ramachandran, Ashwin. "13 Ways to Start a Professional Conversation (With Examples) - Career Advice." Interview Kickstart, April 1, 2024. https://www.interviewkickstart.com/blogs/career-advice/how-to-start-a-conversation.

Raypole, Crystal. "Ready, Set, Journal! 64 Journaling Prompts for Self-Discovery."

Psych Central, September 12, 2016. https://psychcentral.com/blog/ready-set-journal-64-journaling-prompts-for-self-discovery.

Raypole, Crystal. "Visualization Meditation: 5 Exercises to Try." Healthline, May 28, 2020. https://www.healthline.com/health/visualization-meditation.

Ryder, Gina. "How to Understand and Read Body Language." Psych Central, October 21, 2021. https://psychcentral.com/health/body-language.

Segal, Jeanne. "Body Language and Nonverbal Communication." HelpGuide.org, November 2, 2018. https://www.helpguide.org/articles/relationships-communication/nonverbal-communication.htm.

Shafir, Hailey, M.Ed, LCMHCS, LCAS, and CCS. "Why Eye Contact Is Important in Communication." SocialSelf, August 26, 2021. https://socialself.com/blog/eye-contact-important/.

Sharma, Deeksha. "Role Play Training at Work: 7 Effective Tips + Sample Situations." Risely (blog), July 5, 2023. https://www.risely.me/role-play-training-at-work/.

Soeiro, Loren. "7 Tips for Getting Through Difficult Conversations." Psychology Today, May 25, 2021. https://www.psychologytoday.com/us/blog/i-hear-you/202105/7-tips-for-getting-through-difficult-conversations.

Sosnoski, Karen. "How to Use Positive Visualization in Your Everyday Life." Psych Central, May 17, 2016. https://psychcentral.com/lib/imagery-in-everyday-life.

Stavraki, Ioanna. "How to Practice Exposure Therapy for Social Anxiety & Worksheets (PDF)." Simply Psychology (blog), March 26, 2024. https://www.simplypsychology.org/exposure-therapy-for-social-anxiety.html.

Storm, Susan. "How to Communicate Effectively with Any Myers-Briggs® Personality Type." Psychology Junkie (blog), May 22, 2017. https://www.psychologyjunkie.com/communicate-effectively-myers-briggs-personality-type/.

The Muse. "30 Brilliant Networking Conversation Starters," February 22, 2018. https://www.themuse.com/advice/30-brilliant-networking-conversation-starters.

The Recovery Village. "Identifying & Coping with Anxiety Triggers | What Triggers Anxiety Attacks?" The Recovery Village Drug and Alcohol Rehab, May 26, 2022. https://www.therecoveryvillage.com/mental-health/anxiety/anxiety-triggers/.

Van Edwards, Vanessa. "Mirroring Body Language: 4 Steps To Successfully Mirror Others." Science of People, August 7, 2015. https://www.scienceofpeople.com/mirroring/.

Vojkovsky, Roland. "Open-Ended Questions: 28 Examples of How to Ask Properly." Customer Happiness Blog, n.d. https://www.nicereply.com/blog/open-ended-questions-examples/.

Watkins, Natalie. "How to Read and Pick Up On Social Cues (As an Adult)." SocialSelf, March 21, 2021. https://socialself.com/blog/read-social-cues/.

Zajac, John. "The Ultimate Guide to Icebreakers (And How To Use Them)." Workelle, April 17, 2023. https://workelle.com/en/blog/culture/the-ultimate-guide-to-icebreakers-and-how-to-use-them.

Zucker, Rebecca. "How to Follow Up with Someone Who's Not Getting Back to You." Harvard Business Review, January 13, 2021. https://hbr.org/2021/01/how-to-follow-up-with-someone-whos-not-getting-back-to-you.

www.ingramcontent.com/pod-product-compliance
Lightning Source LLC
Chambersburg PA
CBHW070341130626
46556CB00007B/2972